SILLY SOUP

Also by Carol Korty

Plays from African Folktales

SILLY SOUP

TEN ZANY PLAYS

with songs and ideas
for making them your own

CAROL KORTY

PHOTOGRAPHS BY JAMIE COPE

MUSIC BY
Mary Lynn Solot

CHARLES SCRIBNER'S SONS
New York

The lyrics to songs on pages 13, 59, 71, 91, and 101 are based on rhymes in *The Oxford Dictionary of Nursery Rhymes* (1951), edited by Iona and Peter Opie, and are used with the permission of Oxford University Press.

Library of Congress Cataloging in Publication Data

Korty, Carol
   Silly soup.
   Bibliography: p. 145
   SUMMARY: Short nonsensical plays based on the "noodlehead" tales embodied in numerous folk traditions. Includes sections on music, dance, scenery, props, and related topics.
     1. Children's plays.   [1. Plays]   I. Cope, Jamie.
II. Title.
PN6120.A5K7135   812′.5′4   77-23102
ISBN 0-684-15171-5

Dedicated to
the foolishness which keeps us
from being too perfect to be human

ACKNOWLEDGMENTS

There are many people to thank for helping me with these scripts. Nobody makes theater alone. First my thanks go to people for being silly some of the time instead of always serious or sad or responsible. Then thanks to the story tellers who told these wonderful tales about our foolishness in such a beautiful way that they're still true today. Thanks to the six actors who originally worked with me to shape these stories into plays: Martin A. David, William Finley, Danny Goldman, Mark Hammer, Vene Spencer, and Frank Scott. Thanks to Wilford Leach and John Braswell, who helped and encouraged me as a writer and a director. Thanks to Arthur Sainer, who made the space available for the work to happen. Thanks to Sarah Lawrence College for believing that people need to grow in their own way. And thanks to Anne Diven, who first wished to make the plays available to young people through this book.

CONTENTS

SILLY SOUP

ABOUT THESE PLAYS

The plays in this book are about noodles or noodle-heads—happy, zany simpletons who do outlandishly crazy things with the utmost seriousness. A noodlehead is that person, familiar to all of us, who cannot grasp more than one idea at a time. A noodle is that part of us which takes over when common sense abandons us. Try seeing the world from one narrow perspective, with one fixed idea. What have you got? Your noodlehead self—silly, wacky, and ridiculous. This foolish part of us is presented here in the spirit of fun so we can laugh at ourselves together.

Once you start looking for noodlehead behavior, you'll see it everywhere. No one invented it. It must have always been with us. Stories about this very particular kind of foolishness have existed for hundreds of years the world over. You'll find them in folk tales from England, Poland, Turkey, Ethiopia, India, China. Despite the cultural differences, the style of humor is the same.

I picked what struck me as some of the funniest noodlehead stories, mainly from traditional tales about the Mad Merry Men of Gotham, which originated in medieval England, and about the Wise Men of Chelm of Polish Yiddish culture. And I found six very funny people who wanted to act out the stories. We worked together, experimenting and changing, until the stories became the plays that are in this book. In some cases the plot lines are very close to the original stories. In others only the kernel of the joke is the same. What is important is that we made them our own. The plays reflected us. We were in them as characters and as actors, and I think it's because we loved doing them so much that the audience loved seeing them.

Now it's your turn to have fun with them in any way you want. The plays are presented here as a silly soup, that is, a collection of silliness from which you can pick and choose, either to act out scenes for your own fun or to enjoy preparing them to share with an audience. The ingredients are all short pieces no longer than five or ten minutes each. Mix them up in any order you want. There are too many to handle at one sitting, so select the plays and songs you like best and play them in an order that feels right for your occasion.

The characters can be either male or female. They can be those indicated in the scripts or ones you make up yourself. You could act out the plays with only three or four people or with a group as large as your whole school class. The words the characters speak can be the dialogue written here, or your actors could improvise their own words. Don't let memorizing lines become a problem for you. Make up your own words if that's easier or more fun. The ideas in the plays are the important part: zany characters working out wacky solutions to common problems.

In the back of the book is a section with ideas for setting up your scenes, creating comic characters, performing for an audience, using music, making simple sets and costumes. These ideas may help you as you turn the plays into your own pieces. However you use them, be sure they're fun and alive for yourself. The stories will be true for all time if the person telling them or the actors acting them believe in them at that very moment.

THEATER TERMS

To act—to behave as yourself or someone else, doing things in a way that will tell a story through your body and/or voice.

Actor or Player—a person who acts out things with his or her body and/or voice.

Ad-lib—to make up words or action to express a particular response requested by the playwright, such as, "Ad-lib cries of greeting." Similar to improvising but usually meaning only a very short section of improvising within a script.

Character—a person, animal, or object who exists in the play and is brought to life by the actor.

Dialogue—words spoken by the characters in a play.

A freeze—a statue-like pose of one or more actors; it can have a design that is planned in advance or just be a moment when motion is suspended in mid-action.

Improvising—making up things right on the spot. You can improvise acting, dance, or music. When performers improvise, they are creating much or all of their own material without being told what to do by a playwright, choreographer, or composer.

A play—a term sometimes used to mean a script but usually meaning the whole event of acting out and performing a script. Plays can also be made from ideas that are not written out in a script. They can be made up or improvised at the moment they are being performed.

Plot or Plot line—the outline of events that occur with a group of characters in a play or story.

Props—an abbreviation for properties. These are objects the characters use in the action of the play. Hand props are objects small enough to be held by the actors. Bigger pieces such as chairs and sign posts are called stage props or set props; they are part of the scenery.

Rehearsing—the practicing done by actors, dancers, and musicians to get ready for a performance.

Scene—a division of a play that concerns action happening in one physical place and dealing with one main idea. When the characters move to a new place or deal with a new issue, they are beginning a new scene.

Scenery—the things used to dress the performing area. It can be drapes or designs that create an interesting atmosphere or platforms and blocks providing levels and places from which to make entrances and exits. It can also be things to make the area look like a particular place such as an inn or a street.

A script—the words of the play written by the playwright, including dialogue and stage directions.

A set—the performing area for the play, complete with all the scenery.

To set—to choose one particular way of doing an action,

saying a line, playing some music, in order to repeat it in just that manner each time the piece is played.

Stage—the place where the action of a play is rehearsed or performed. It can be the stage in an auditorium or any open space that actors set aside to use as the performing area. It might be in a classroom, a living room, an empty lot, or a backyard. (See page 137.)

Stage directions—instructions written by the playwright to help the actors know what the characters are doing; stage directions also often describe the character and the physical setting on stage. (In this book they are set off from the dialogue by italic type and are enclosed in parentheses.)

THE CHARACTERS

CLOWN is bossy, very sure of him/herself, and almost always wrong.

CLYDE is sweet-tempered, giggly, and preoccupied with things very close to him/herself.

EXTREMELY LONG is extremely long, in love with him/herself, and haughty toward others.

SMALL is innocent, busy, and optimistic.

TALL is fussy, precise, excitable, and effusive.

The characters can be either male or female. Those indicated for each of the plays don't have to be the characters to do that play; feel free to use different combinations. Use as many or as few characters as fit your needs. Five are given here, but you could act out most of the plays with three people, having the same characters appear in all of your pieces. You could also use many actors, having different characters for each play. Either way you'd be creating the feeling of a town of zanies. (You'll notice that the children in the photographs often added or changed characters in a given script.)

However many characters you use, make each one a distinct personality, different from the others. Find a name that fits each well, and check to see that your whole group has interesting variety.

OPENING AND TRANSITIONS

If you're doing several of these pieces as a presentation for an audience, it's a good idea to have some kind of introduction of your characters at the start because they probably won't all be seen in the first play. You could introduce them through one of the songs, through a little dance, or with some silly walks and greetings.

The plays are short; each ends sharply by completing the joke that was set up during the scene. To help this comic format, work out a simple, snappy way to get into and out of each scene. By repeating this method for each of your changes, you will establish a bit of formality which will be a nice contrast to the craziness within each of the scenes.

One way to do this is to have the noodle characters take turns making the introductions. Or there could be a silent group freeze (see page 4), with characters holding signs that announce each scene. Another way would be to have the scene start with all its characters running or dancing out. They set up the props; on the same count they make a group statue; each says his or her name; together they say the title of the piece; then they break the freeze and immediately start the action.

You could also choose to use a Master of Ceremonies (an M.C.) who would introduce the pieces to the audience, much as you'd have at a circus or a variety show on television. The M.C. might even enter the action in certain places as a non-noodle, who loves the noodles nonetheless. He might take the role of an innkeeper or in *Building the House* the person passing through. He or she might even join *Moon Shot,* be drawn into the characters' logic, and become one of them in the end!

THE PLAYS AND SONGS

"HEY, DIDDLE, DIDDLE"

This song could be used as your opening number and sung again at the close of your show. You might find it fun to do a little dance with it, too—or it could be used between any of the talky plays where you'd like a change of pace.

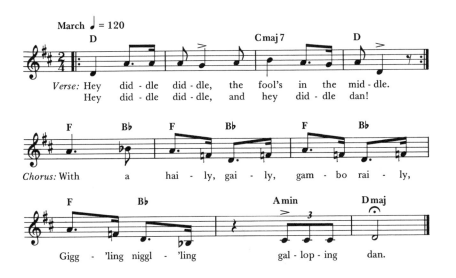

Verse 2: Hig-ge-dy dicket, and pig-ged-dy, pop!
   Cat's in a flur-ry; the dog ate the mop.
Chorus: With a, etc.

Verse 3: Han-dy, a dan-dy; sing ric-ket o ran-dy.
   Give us a song with a rid-dle-dy ro.
Chorus: With a, etc.

13

BAG OF GOLD

Characters:	Props:
CLOWN	large, sturdy bag
CLYDE	gold-colored bricks
TALL as INNKEEPER	Inn sign
	2 chairs
	bed headboard (*to attach to chairs*)
	bed footboard (*attached to bench or stools*)
	thin, flat paper bags

(CLOWN, CLYDE, and TALL *run out, set up a three-person freeze, and announce themselves.*)

CLOWN: Clown,

CLYDE: Clyde,

TALL: and Tall in . . .

ALL: *Bag of Gold.*
(TALL *exits to one side and* CLOWN *and* CLYDE *to the other, to quickly re-enter struggling with a large, heavy bag.*)

CLOWN: Come on, Clyde, bring the bag of gold over here. We've got to get it home tonight.

CLYDE: Whew . . . I'm trying. It's so heavy!

CLOWN: This is the heaviest bag of gold I ever carried.

CLYDE: This gold is heavier than feathers.

CLOWN. I never knew gold was so heavy, or I wouldn't have volunteered to take it. (*They stop for a moment to rest.*)

CLYDE: Whew! I hope we can get it home all right.

CLOWN: Hey, Clyde, do you want to take a look at the gold?

CLYDE: Yes, let's.

CLOWN: Come on, take a peek at it. (*They do.*) Boy, that is pretty!

CLYDE: That is the most beautiful gold I've ever seen. Look how it shines in the sun. (*Each pulls out a brick or two to admire it.*)

CLOWN: Say, I bet robbers would really love to steal this.

CLYDE: They sure would.

CLOWN: Robbers!

CLYDE: Robbers! (*They shove bricks back into bag.*)

CLOWN: Quick, hide it. Hide the (*spelling it out*) g-o-l-d.

CLYDE: G-o-l-d? What's that?

CLOWN: That's what's in the bag.

CLYDE: Oh, the gold!

CLOWN: Shhhhh. Don't say that. Say g-o-l-d.

CLYDE: G-o-l-d.

CLOWN: Now we have to be on the lookout for robbers. Where do robbers like to rob?

CLYDE: Where do robbers like to rob?

CLOWN: Robbers like to rob where it is very dark and where there are no people around.

CLYDE: Robbers like to rob where it is very dark and where there are no people around. Oh, well, it is very light here. Look how lovely and light.

CLOWN: It's a good thing, too. Clyde . . .

CLYDE: Yes.

CLOWN: Do you see any people around?

CLYDE: Let me look. Uh-oh. Now that you mention it . . .

CLOWN (*pointing to empty area around them*): Clyde, look!

CLYDE: What?

CLOWN: There's nobody there.

CLYDE: I know. There're no people around here.

CLOWN: That's where robbers like to rob! (*Both react with fear.*) Get the g-o-l-d. Let's get out of here.

CLYDE: Okay.

CLOWN: Come on. Come on. Let's go.

CLYDE: I'm getting it.

CLOWN: What's the matter?

CLYDE (*struggling alone*): It's very heavy.

CLOWN: It's too heavy?

CLYDE: Too heavy.

CLOWN: I have an idea. It's too heavy for you to carry *and* to walk. So you just carry the gold, and I will carry you.

CLYDE: Okay.

CLOWN: Have you got a good grip? (CLOWN *picks up* CLYDE, *who tries to pick up the bag again but drops it.*)

CLYDE: Oh, that's much better! This I like.

CLOWN (*seeing bag is still on ground*): This won't do. The gold is just too heavy for you. *I'll* carry the gold, and you carry me.

CLYDE: Now, that's smart!

CLOWN (*picking up bag*): All right. Carry me.

CLYDE (*walking around looking for a good angle*): I'm getting ready.

CLOWN: All right, come on.

CLYDE: I think I'm ready.

CLOWN: I'm ready, too.

CLYDE: Okay.

CLOWN: Come on. Carry me.

CLYDE: I'm ready. (*Grabs him around knees and tries unsuccessfully to budge him.*)

CLOWN: Lift me up.

CLYDE: Okay. (*Tries from another ridiculous angle.*)

CLOWN: Just a little bit higher, I think.

CLYDE: All right. (*Steps back, runs and jumps up, grabbing* CLOWN *around shoulders, and falls to ground.*)

CLOWN: It's not going to work. (*Drops bag.*) We're never going to get home this way. We're simply too tired. We'll have to go some place and stay overnight. And tomorrow morning, when we're all rested, we'll be able to carry it.

CLYDE: Yes, then we'll be strong enough to carry it. Where shall we go?

CLOWN: We've got to go *in* someplace to stay clear of robbers.

CLYDE: Yes, right in.

CLOWN: You're right, an inn.
(INNKEEPER *enters on one side and puts out an Inn sign.*)

CLOWN: Oh, there's one! Come on. (*They drag bag.*) But listen, don't tell anybody what's in the bag.

CLYDE: What's in the bag? You mean the gold?

CLOWN: Ah, ah, ah . . . shhhhh. Don't tell anyone about the g-o-l-d.

CLYDE: Right. (*They approach the Inn.*) Hello!

INNKEEPER: Oh, hello, hello there.

CLOWN: We would like a place to spend the night.

INNKEEPER: Well, you have come to the right place! (*Immediately noticing the bag.*) What do you have in the bag?

CLOWN: What aaaaaa . . . . (*The two quickly back up.* CLOWN *takes off his hat and puts it on the bag.*) This is a friend of ours. His name is G-o-l-d. And we would like a place for the three of us to stay overnight.

INNKEEPER (*growing more curious about the bag*): Your friend is very small. He must have smoked when he was young. Well, come on in and sit down. (CLOWN *and* CLYDE *sit with the bag at their feet.*) Would you like another chair for your friend?

CLOWN: No, no.

CLYDE: No. He's fine right here by us. Say, do you have any robbers here?

INNKEEPER: Robbers? In my inn? Certainly not.

CLOWN: Well, don't send out for any, because we don't want them.

CLYDE: You know, these chairs are very uncomfortable.

CLOWN: They are indeed hard. Innkeeper, since we're going to stay all night, would you mind getting rid of these very hard chairs and bringing us a nice soft bed, please?

CLYDE: A nice, soft bed.

INNKEEPER: Well, beds are very expensive in this part of the country. Do you have any money to pay for a bed?

CLOWN: Money?

CLYDE: Money? Clown, I don't have any money. Do you?

CLOWN (*to* INNKEEPER): Well, no, we don't have any money exactly, but would you consider accepting a piece of . . . say . . . gold?

INNKEEPER (*eagerly*): Gold? Do you have gold?

CLOWN & CLYDE: No, no, no.

CLOWN: We, ourselves, don't actually have gold, but perhaps our friend here might have a stray piece or two.

CLYDE: He may have some.

CLOWN (*looking into bag*): Pardon me, do you happen to have . . . (*Takes out a brick.*) Thank you very much. (*To* INNKEEPER.) There you are, my good woman. Buy yourself a yacht.

INNKEEPER (*taking her brick greedily*): Stay right here. I'll have your bed in a minute. (*She exits.*)

CLYDE: Thank you. Clown, you know, these chairs are so uncomfortable. I'm just dreaming of a nice, soft, downy bed. (INNKEEPER *returns, puts a headboard on the back of their chairs. Exits again.*)

CLOWN: It will be very nice to get a bed.

CLYDE: We'll wake up in the morning refreshed. Am I tired!

CLOWN: We'll get off these hard chairs and into a nice soft bed, and tomorrow morning we'll wake up and be all strong and ready to carry the g-o-l-d.
(INNKEEPER *brings in foot of the bed; it could be a bench with a bed footboard painted or built on the side facing the audience or any other set prop made to look like a bed.*)

CLOWN & CLYDE (*putting their feet on bench and settling down*): Ahhhhhhh.

INNKEEPER: There you are.

CLYDE: This is much better.

23

CLOWN: Very comfortable, indeed.

INNKEEPER: I'll tell you what. Down the hall, I have a little room with a little bed that would be just right for your friend. I'll just take him down there.

CLOWN & CLYDE: No, no, no!

CLYDE: He's very shy and afraid at night.

CLOWN: He likes to stay right with us.

INNKEEPER: All right. Well, sleep tight, fellows. Pleasant dreams. If you need anything else, don't hesitate to call on me.

CLOWN: Thank you and, if you need anything, you just call on us.
(INNKEEPER exits.)

CLYDE: I'm so tired, Clown, that I'm falling asleep already, and my eyes are closed.

CLOWN: My eyes are closing, too. Oh, wait. We can't both go to sleep. One of us has to watch the g-o-l-d.

CLYDE: Okay, you watch, and I'll sleep.

CLOWN: Okay, I'll watch, and you sleep.

CLYDE: Okay, I'm sleeping.

CLOWN: Okay, I'm watching.

CLYDE: Good.

CLOWN: Clyde!

CLYDE: What?

CLOWN: Are you sleeping?

CLYDE: Yes, I'm still sleeping.

CLOWN: Good, I'm watching.

CLYDE: Boy, am I sleeping.

CLOWN: Boy, am I watching. Hey, Clyde, did you close the door?

CLYDE: No, I didn't close the door.

CLOWN: Better get up and close the door.

CLYDE: I can't close the door. I'm sleeping.

CLOWN: Well, I can't close the door. I'm watching. Someone has to close the door, or robbers might come in.

CLYDE: I can't do it because I'm sleeping.

CLOWN: Well, I can't do it because I'm watching.

CLYDE: (*rousing himself*): Wait, I have an idea. We'll play a game. We'll both close our eyes, and the first person to open his eyes will have to close the door. Okay?

CLOWN: Okay. We'll both close our eyes. One, two, three, close. Your eyes closed?

CLYDE: My eyes are closed. Are yours closed?

CLOWN: Yes, let me see yours. (*He opens his eyes to look.*) Yeh, they're closed.

CLYDE: Okay. Are your eyes closed?

CLOWN: Yes.

CLYDE: Let me see. (*He turns to look with his eyes*

closed.) Okay, they're closed. Hey, Clown, you know, it's awfully dark in here with my eyes closed.

CLOWN: It *is* very dark. Ohhh . . . Clyde, where do robbers like to rob?

CLYDE: Robbers like to rob where it is very dark . . .

CLOWN & CLYDE (*scuffling for the bag with eyes still shut:*) I've got it. Where is it? Give it to me.

CLOWN: Wait. We'll take turns.
(ROBBER *enters behind them with a cape over her head. It is the* INNKEEPER *in disguise.*)

CLYDE: Okay. I have it. It's my turn first. (ROBBER *goes to* CLYDE'S *side of bed to try to take bag.*)

CLOWN: You've got it?

CLYDE: Yes, I have it.

CLOWN: All right, it's my turn now. (ROBBER *crosses behind bed to try from* CLOWN'S *side.*)

CLYDE: All right. Here it is.

CLOWN: Okay. I've got it.

CLYDE: You've got it?

CLOWN: Yes, I have it.

CLYDE: All right. It's my turn now.

CLOWN: Okay, here you go. Have you got it? (ROBBER *crosses back again.*)

CLYDE: I've got it.

CLOWN: Okay.

ROBBER: It's my turn now.

CLYDE: Okay. (*Passes bag to* ROBBER.) You've got it?

ROBBER: I've got it. (*Takes hat off gold, leaves it on headboard, and moves aside to count the gold.*)

CLOWN: Okay, it's my turn now. Give it to me.

CLYDE: Uh-oh! I don't have it, Clown. I just gave it to you.

CLOWN: No, you didn't. I gave it to you.

CLYDE: Where is it?

CLOWN: We better open our eyes quickly. Ready? One, two, three, open. (*Seeing it with* ROBBER.) Oh, there it is!

CLYDE: I thought we'd lost it.

CLOWN (*crossing to* ROBBER): Excuse me, madam; that belongs to us. (*Takes gold from her.*) (ROBBER *starts to sneak off.*) (*To* CLYDE.) Wait a minute. We both opened our eyes at the same time. Who's going to close the door?

CLYDE: I don't know.

28

CLOWN (*calling after* ROBBER): Hey! (ROBBER *stops in her tracks.*) Would you mind closing the door on your way out?

ROBBER: Certainly. (*Runs off, closing door.*) (CLOWN *and* CLYDE *get back into bed.*)

CLOWN: Boy, that was lucky. We got our gold back, and now we'll get the door closed.

CLYDE: Yes, that is a relief. I thought we had lost it.

CLOWN: Say, Clyde, who was that who just closed the door?

CLYDE: I don't know; I never saw her before in my whole life.

CLOWN: It was probably just some robber. (*Freezes.*) Robber!

CLYDE: Robber!

CLOWN: Robbers! We're going to have to get rid of this gold. It gives us nothing but trouble.

CLYDE: I never liked it. Let's get rid of it.

CLOWN: We better give it away, because if we don't give it away, it will be stolen from us.

CLYDE: Well, we can't just give it away to somebody; they'd get suspicious.

CLOWN: I know, we'll sell it! We'll sell it for something robbers wouldn't want to rob.

CLYDE: That's a good idea . . . for something robbers wouldn't want to rob. Call the innkeeper.

CLOWN: Innkeeper!

INNKEEPER (*running in*): You called?

CLOWN: My partner and I would like to do some business with you.

INNKEEPER: Business? Very good.

CLOWN: We have some gold which we would like to sell.

INNKEEPER: Oh, I don't have enough money to buy gold.

CLOWN & CLYDE: Money!

CLOWN: No, no. We don't want any money.

INNKEEPER: You don't want money?

CLOWN & CLYDE: No.

INNKEEPER: How about diamonds?

CLOWN & CLYDE: No.

CLYDE: Diamonds! No. We couldn't even spell diamonds.

CLOWN: We want something that robbers wouldn't want.

INNKEEPER: I know something robbers wouldn't want. Garbage.

CLYDE: Ugh. But we don't even want that ourselves. Who likes garbage?

INNKEEPER: Well, down in the cellar, I have a stack of paper bags.

CLOWN & CLYDE: Paper bags! Perfect.

INNKEEPER: I'll go get them. (*Runs off laughing.*)

CLOWN: Oh, are we smart! (*Laughing.*) We'll give her the gold, and she'll give us the bags. And then, when the robbers come to steal the gold, they won't steal it from us . . .

CLYDE: . . . they'll steal it from her. Oh, delicious paper bags.

INNKEEPER (*running in with bags*): Here are the paper bags.

CLOWN: And here is your bag of gold. Thank you very much.

INNKEEPER: Thank you very much. It's a pleasure doing business with you. (*She exits with gold.*) (CLYDE *takes bags and moves away to look them over.*)

CLOWN: Boy, were we smart! She was so stupid. I knew that she was stupid when I first saw her. (*Chuckles.*)

CLYDE: Clown.

CLOWN: Yes.

CLYDE: You know, I don't like to mention this, but maybe we weren't so smart.

CLOWN: Is that possible?

CLYDE: It's possible. You know we gave that innkeeper a big, fat bag bulging with gold, and all we have are little, skinny paper bags.

CLOWN: You're right. Empty bags. We've been cheated. Wait a minute. Wait a minute! Innkeeper! (*To* CLYDE.) Let me handle this.

CLYDE: Yes.
(INNKEEPER *runs in.*)

CLOWN: We don't like to complain about the service, but it seems to me that we have been cheated. We gave you a big bag full of gold, and you gave us nothing but empty paper bags. Now fill them up with something, please. (*He hands them over.*)

INNKEEPER: You want me to fill them up with something?

CLOWN & CLYDE: Yes.

INNKEEPER: Money?

CLOWN & CLYDE: No!

INNKEEPER: Diamonds?

CLOWN & CLYDE: No!

INNKEEPER: Garbage?

CLOWN & CLYDE: Definitely not.

INNKEEPER: You want them filled with something that robbers wouldn't want? I know. (*She picks up a bag, scoops up air with it, and twists the top closed.*) We can fill them with air.

CLOWN & CLYDE: Yes, with air!

CLOWN: Who would want to steal air?

CLYDE: And it's so easy to carry! (*They all busy themselves filling the bags.*)

CLOWN (*to* INNKEEPER): Hey, no cheating. Fill them up to the top.

INNKEEPER: Do you have another bag? There's a little bit left over up there. (*She fills last bag.*)

CLOWN: All right. Thank you very much. It was a pleasure doing business with you.

INNKEEPER: It was a pleasure doing business with you. (*She quickly removes the foot and head of bed and the Inn sign as the scene finishes.*)

CLOWN: Boy, did we outsmart her! (*Chuckling as they gather up the bags.*) She's stuck with that big, heavy bag of gold that the robbers will steal, and we have all these beautiful, light bags filled with air!

CLYDE: Paper bags filled with genuine air! Nice, light, fluffy air! Oh, boy! (*He pops several bags.*) Were we smart!

(*Both exit gleefully tossing the bags.*)

CLEVER CLYDE

Characters:	*Props:*

CLOWN as Master of
  Ceremonies
	hoop (*or any props needed*
	  for your tricks)

SMALL	instruments or noisemakers
CLYDE	for fanfare
TALL (*optional*)	2 chairs (*optional*)
EXTREMELY LONG (*optional*)	drum and drumsticks

Note: This piece is about an announcer and a trainer enthusiastically presenting a performer in a series of tricks which the performer never really does. In their excitement, neither SMALL nor CLOWN notices that CLYDE isn't doing more than one trick. The act will work with any set of tricks that you want to use. In picking them, make sure each one SMALL does is a little more difficult or interesting than the last, so there will be a build in excitement. The actor playing CLYDE, of course, doesn't have to be able to do more than one—or maybe not even one; he could just giggle. The joke could work in a number of ways: CLYDE could be very silly or giggly or easily distracted; he could be shy and too embarrassed to move; he could be hopelessly confused and trying to cover up for it. Find the circumstance that is funniest for your particular actors. In all cases, SMALL is so excited for

CLYDE that, once they're underway, she never notices what he is really doing.

Fanfare suggestion: Calliope music could be playing in the background throughout to give a circus feeling. Your extra actors could sit on chairs at the side and play a spurt of sound on noisemakers or instruments after each trick. They could also play a drum roll as build-up before each trick. Or the Master of Ceremonies (M.C.) could play the drum roll himself, as he announces each trick.

(*Calliope music starts;* TALL *and* EXTREMELY LONG *enter with chairs and instruments and sit ready to play.*) (*Drum roll.*)

M.C. (entering with a flourish): Ladies and Gentlemen, the Merry Fools and Noodles present for your pleasure the amazing tricks of Clever Clyde. Ladies and Gentlemen, it's Clever Clyde! (*Fanfare.*) (SMALL *runs out.*) . . . and his trainer, Small. Take a bow, Clyde and Small! (*Drum roll and fanfare.*)

SMALL: Clyde, come on out. (*To audience.*) He's a little shy, you know. (*Coaxing him out.*) You mustn't be shy, Clyde. Here he is! Isn't he terrific? He's all ready. (CLYDE *moves away and hides his face.*) Oh, come on, Clyde. These are very nice people. They're all pulling for you. (*He inches back.*) All right, he's ready now.

M.C.: He is ready?

SMALL: Yes, he's ready.

M.C.: The first trick will be . . .

SMALL: The roll-over.

M.C.: . . . The Roll-Over!

SMALL: Clyde, the roll-over? (*To audience.*) Oh, I think he's forgotten it. (*To* CLYDE.) Shall I remind you how it goes? (CLYDE *nods.*) Watch very closely. It goes like this. One, two, three, roll over. (*She does it.*) Da, Da! (*Fanfare.*) Okay? (CLYDE *looks embarrassed.*) Well, we'll do a different one then. Let's try the tap step. It goes like this (*Demonstrating*). Remember? No? Shall I break it down for you? Watch closely now. (*She starts to do it slowly, and* CLYDE *whips it off behind her.*) Hey! Do that again. (*He repeats.*) (*Fanfare.*) Marvelous! He's really getting warmed up. Isn't he great? Now . . . (*She runs to get a hoop.*)

M.C.: Ladies and Gentlemen, presenting The Hoop!

SMALL: He loves this trick. It really is his favorite. Come on, Clyde. Through the hoop. Clyde, come on. Here he goes!
(*Drum roll as* CLYDE *backs up and runs forward to jump through. He stops just short, freezes a second, and does his tap step.*) (*Fanfare.*) (SMALL

doesn't notice he hasn't gone through and puts aside hoop.) Isn't he marvelous? How about this one? (*She does a little split jump caper.*) I love this one myself. I'll do it with you. Come on. (*She takes his hand and does the step while* CLYDE *just stands.*) Terrific! Now the gallop. (*She gallops around him in a circle a couple times, exiting with it.*) Faster! Faster! (CLYDE *stands in awkward silence. He does his tap step again, looking pleased.*) (*Fanfare.*) (CLYDE *runs off; drum roll as* CLOWN *follows.* EXTREMELY LONG *and* TALL *clear the chairs and instruments.*)

OPERA SINGER

Characters:	Props:
EXTREMELY LONG	3 chairs
CLOWN	large cardboard with bathtub
SMALL	painted on the side
	hammer and metal pipe
	hammer and wooden box
	2 sign posts
	4 signs: Plumber
	Carpenter
	Empty
	Vacant

(EXTREMELY LONG, CLOWN, *and* SMALL *zip on, form a three-person freeze, and announce themselves.*)

EXTREMELY LONG: Extremely Long,

CLOWN: Clown,

SMALL: and Small in . . .

ALL: *Opera Singer.*
(CLOWN *and* SMALL *exit to bring in their chairs and signs.* CLOWN *sets up his Plumber's shop on one side of the stage, and* SMALL *sets up her Carpenter's shop on the other side while* EXTREMELY LONG *begins the scene in the center.*)

40

EXTREMELY LONG (*vocalizing*): Mi, mi, mi. What a beautiful voice! (*To audience.*) Good afternoon, dear people. You have the pleasure to witness the great opera singer, me, practicing in my bath, as is my custom. Pardon me, please, while I make preparations. (*He continues to vocalize while setting up the cardboard bathtub against a chair, turning on and adjusting the water.*) Beautiful! Exquisite! (*He takes off coat and "steps into tub," sitting on chair behind the cardboard. When his singing is going strong,* CARPENTER *begins to hammer.* EXTREMELY LONG *first tries to incorporate the tempo with his singing, but when the* PLUMBER *also begins to hammer,* EXTREMELY LONG *finds it impossible.*)

EXTREMELY LONG: I cannot hear myself sing! This noise is terrible. It must stop! (*He gets out of tub, wraps coat around his waist, goes next door to the Plumber's shop, and knocks on imaginary door. During the next dialogue,* SMALL *tones down her hammering.*) Knocka, knocka, knocka.

CLOWN: What?

EXTREMELY LONG: Pardon me, sir.

CLOWN: What?

EXTREMELY LONG: Will you please be quiet in there? You are making too much noise.

CLOWN: I can't hear you. I'm making too much noise.

41

EXTREMELY LONG: Exactly. Would you please stop? Stop! (PLUMBER *stops*.) Thank you.

CLOWN: Why do you want me to stop?

EXTREMELY LONG: Because I am a great opera singer, and I practice right next door in my bath.

CLOWN: So?

EXTREMELY LONG: With your banging on your pipe, I cannot hear myself sing.

CLOWN: What do you want to hear yourself sing for?

EXTREMELY LONG: Because my voice is beautiful!

CLOWN: What do you want me to do about it?

EXTREMELY LONG: I would like you to stop your banging and move your shop so that I can practice in peace.

CLOWN: Move my shop?

EXTREMELY LONG: Yes.

CLOWN: Wait a minute. Wait a minute. You're an opera singer?

EXTREMELY LONG: That is correct.

CLOWN: And you live right next door?

EXTREMELY LONG: I do.

CLOWN: And you practice in your bath?

EXTREMELY LONG: That's right!

CLOWN: Boy, I'm moving to another shop. If I lived next door to an opera singer, I couldn't hear myself pound!

EXTREMELY LONG: Bravissimo! He is going to move. I will have silence. (*Returns to tub and starts to get in.* CARPENTER *begins to pound loudly.*

43

EXTREMELY LONG *goes over to her shop. During this dialogue,* CLOWN *takes his time to pack up his shop and change* Plumber *sign to* Vacant *sign.)*

EXTREMELY LONG (*in falsetto*): Knocka, knocka, knocka.

SMALL (*stops*): Yes, yes.

EXTREMELY LONG: Pardon me, Dear Little Person.

SMALL: Yes.

EXTREMELY LONG: You are making too much noise with your tipa tipa tipa tip!

SMALL: Well, I'm sorry, but I've got to get this job finished by tonight. It's my living, you know.

EXTREMELY LONG: But then I cannot hear myself sing.

SMALL: Oh.

EXTREMELY LONG: And what is more important: my magnificent golden voice or your insignificant little brown box?

SMALL: Ah . . . your magnificent golden voice?

EXTREMELY LONG: Correct!

SMALL: Well, what do you suggest I do about this?

EXTREMELY LONG: How much money would be

44

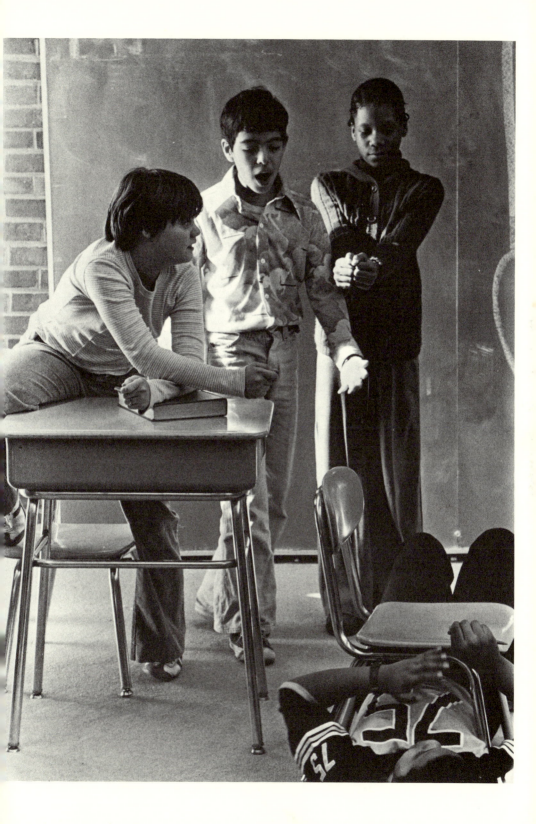

necessary to convince you to move? (*Pulls out a roll of bills.*)

SMALL: Hey, with all that money, I could get a bigger shop, couldn't I?

EXTREMELY LONG: You certainly could!

SMALL: Oh, yes, I think I'll move right away.

EXTREMELY LONG: Congratulations.

SMALL: Thank you.

EXTREMELY LONG: Good shopping.

SMALL: Happy singing! (*Chuckles to herself while taking down* Carpenter *sign and putting up* Empty *sign.*)

EXTREMELY LONG: *Arrivederci!* Ah, silence at last. Back to my bath. (*He gets into tub and settles down while* SMALL *and* CLOWN *cross to other sides of stage, without seeing each other.*)

CLOWN: I'm going to find a new shop.

SMALL: I'm going to get a better shop. Somewhere along this avenue. This neighborhood has been very kind to me. (*Seeing* CLOWN's *old shop.*) Vacant! Here's a place.

CLOWN (*seeing* SMALL's *old shop*): Empty! Here's a good shop. How lucky! (*As they set up their new shops,* EXTREMELY LONG *begins to sing again. Loud pounding takes over.*)

46

EXTREMELY LONG: No, no! This is impossible. (*Shouting over the hammering.*) I cannot hear my own voice. I will have to give up singing. I must take up something silent. Something rhythmic. I will take up the dance! It is much better. I don't have to hear myself now. (*He exits with dance steps while holding his bathtub in front of him.*)

(TALL *or* CLYDE *or both could enter with drum or noisemakers to clear* SMALL *and* CLOWN *off the stage.*)

CLOWN: Say, can you hold it down a little?

(*All exit with their props.*) (*This is a good place for characters to sing "Hey, Diddle, Diddle" if you haven't used it as an opening.*)

JOGGING

Characters:	*Props:*
TALL	bench
CLYDE	2 pairs of different shoes, one with higher heel or platform sole

(*An actor runs out and places a bench in the middle of the stage.* TALL *and* CLYDE *jog across.* TALL *is wearing two different shoes, one heel higher than the other. They freeze and announce themselves.*)

TALL: Tall

CLYDE: and Clyde in . . .

BOTH: *Jogging. (They continue jogging back and forth during their dialogue.)*

TALL (*limping*): It is a lovely day for a jog.

CLYDE: I love it.

TALL: But watch out for this road.

CLYDE (*looking around while jogging*): What's wrong with the road?

TALL: Bumps. It's very uneven.

48

CLYDE (*circling*): I don't feel bumps.

TALL: There're lots of them. It's all up, down, up, down.

CLYDE: No, it's not. Look at it. It's straight. (*Stopping her.*) See, I jog straight, straight, straight.

TALL (*jogging again*): Well, it makes me jog crooked, crooked, crooked.

CLYDE (*catching up*): Tall . . .

TALL (*stops and turns to look at him*): Maybe something's wrong with you.

CLYDE: It's *you* who's jogging crooked.

TALL: Oh! (*Becoming worried.*) Oh, dear.

CLYDE: Shall I have a look?

TALL: Yes, please do. Don't be afraid to tell me the worst.

CLYDE (*looking under her jacket*): Well, this part seems to be all right.

TALL: I knew it wasn't me.

CLYDE: Maybe it's your legs. (*Going to the bench.*) Stand up here. We'll have a look. (*He pulls up each pants leg.*) This one looks all right. And this one is fine, too.

TALL: Yes, my legs are fine. You see, they each go from my belt down to the bench.

CLYDE: How about your feet?

TALL: Well, this one in the black shoe feels fine . . .

CLYDE: Nice shoe, too.

TALL: . . . and so does the foot in the yellow shoe.

CLYDE: Hmmmmm.

TALL: Oh, Clyde, the black shoe and the yellow shoe!

CLYDE: What?

TALL: Look! It's not my legs! It's not my feet! It's my shoes! I have on two different shoes.

CLYDE: Oh, for heaven's sake. You silly thing.

TALL: Say, Clyde, would you do me a favor? My other shoes are at home. Would you please run home and bring me my other shoes?

CLYDE: You have other shoes like these?

TALL: Yes, of course. If you get them for me, we can finish our jog.

CLYDE: Sure, I'll get them. (*He runs off.*)

TALL: My, my, my. That's a relief. I thought it was me. It was the shoes! How could I have done such a silly thing? Why, this yellow one doesn't even match my outfit. Sometimes I think I'm a little bit stupid.

CLYDE (*running on with the mate to each shoe* TALL *is wearing*): Here you are, Tall.

TALL: Thank you very much. I'll take off this one which made me walk all crooked and put on this one from home. (*She takes off her black shoe, gives it to* CLYDE *in exchange for a yellow one.*)

CLYDE: What shall I do with it?

TALL: Just throw it away. What a nuisance it was!

CLYDE (*looking it over admiringly*): You don't want it?

TALL: Nooo. (CLYDE *quickly takes off one of his shoes, throws it away, and puts on* TALL's *black shoe.*) (TALL *takes off her yellow shoe.*) And we'll get rid of this one. Give me the other one from home. (CLYDE *gives her the black mate and takes the yellow.*) Throw that one away, too.

CLYDE: But it's a good shoe.

TALL: It made me walk crooked. I don't ever want to see it again. (CLYDE *quickly takes off his other shoe, throws it away, and puts on* TALL's *yellow shoe.*)

TALL: Good, now I'm all set. Are you ready?

CLYDE (*admiring self*): I'm ready.

TALL (*starting up*): Let's finish our jog.

CLYDE (*jogging after her*): How's it now?

TALL: You know. This road is still uneven! (*She jogs off limping.*)

CLYDE (*following with limp*): Yeh, I see what you mean. (*Exits looking about perplexed.*)

THE PUMPKIN

<table>
<tr><td>Characters:</td><td>Props:</td></tr>
<tr><td>SMALL</td><td>a bench</td></tr>
<tr><td>CLYDE</td><td>2 chairs</td></tr>
<tr><td>EXTREMELY LONG</td><td>a pumpkin (artificial or real</td></tr>
<tr><td>CLOWN as INNKEEPER</td><td>one scooped out)</td></tr>
<tr><td></td><td>Inn sign</td></tr>
<tr><td></td><td>short rope</td></tr>
<tr><td></td><td>broom</td></tr>
</table>

(SMALL, CLYDE, CLOWN, *and* EXTREMELY LONG *run on, form a four-person freeze focusing on* SMALL, *who holds a pumpkin, and announce themselves.*)

CLYDE: Clyde,

CLOWN: Clown,

EXTREMELY LONG: Extremely Long,

SMALL: and Small in . . .

ALL: *The Pumpkin.*
(EXTREMELY LONG *and* CLOWN *set up a bench and a chair on one side of the stage.* EXTREMELY LONG *sits on the bench, staying in a quiet pose during the first part of the scene.* CLOWN *exits.* SMALL *and* CLYDE *set up a chair on the other side*

53

of the stage. CLYDE *sits in it, polishing the pump-kin.*)

SMALL (*pacing about*): You know, Clyde, I am rest-less and bored today.

CLYDE: You better find something to do. I'm busy polishing my pumpkin. I'm going to make pie later on.

SMALL: That's marvelous. I wish I had something really interesting to do. Something exciting and different. Oh, let's go to town! I'd love to go to town.

CLYDE: Well, go on.

SMALL: By myself?

CLYDE: Sure, you can go by yourself. I go by myself.

SMALL: Well, golly, I've never been there before, and, if I went by myself, I might lose myself among all those new people.

CLYDE: What do you mean?

SMALL: Well, I know you, and I am used to you, so that when I look at you, I know that that's you, Clyde. And, when I look at me, I know that it's me, Small. But with a lot of new people, I wouldn't be able to tell who was who, and I might lose myself.

CLYDE: Oh. I never really had that problem.

SMALL: If only I had something that would make me look really different from everybody so I could be very sure that it was me.

CLYDE: Yes, something to make you look very different.

SMALL: Say, Clyde.

CLYDE: Yes.

SMALL: When you were to town, did you ever see anyone who went around with a pumpkin all the time?

CLYDE: With a pumpkin? (*Giggles.*) No.

SMALL: Well, if I could tie a pumpkin to me and always have it on me, then, whenever I looked there and saw the pumpkin, I would know that it was me, Small.

CLYDE: Oh, that's a good idea. The person with the pumpkin would be Small.

SMALL: Right.

CLYDE: Where are you going to get a pumpkin?

SMALL: I thought maybe you would lend me yours.

CLYDE: Well, if you take very good care of it. I want it back later to make the pie.

SMALL: Oh, yes, I will be very careful with it. (*Takes a rope out of her pocket.*) Would you help me tie it on my leg? (*They tie the rope onto the pumpkin and her ankle, leaving some slack.*)

CLYDE: I'm not very good at tying.

SMALL: I am an expert tie-er. I tie very well.

CLYDE (*setting pumpkin on floor*): Careful not to squish it.

SMALL: Oh, no, I never would. I guess I'm all set now.

CLYDE: I'll just take a little nap while you are gone.

SMALL: All right. Wish me luck.

CLYDE: Good luck. (*He curls up in chair for a nap.*)

SMALL: Good-bye. Oh, boy, here I go! (*She sets out on a little walking pattern across the stage. After taking a few large steps with pumpkin dragging . . .*) You know, this is harder than I thought it would be. It is very awkward. (*Walks.*) At least I won't get lost and that makes it worth it. But (*stops to comment*)

It's hard for a very small lumpkin
To take a walk with a pumpkin,
Because it makes a bumpkin
Every step of the way.
(*Walks with pumpkin.*)

This pumpkin walks so jerkily,

56

I'd rather walk with a turkily.
(*Stops again to reflect.*)

I think perhaps that some kin
Take a walk with a pumpkin.
If some kin, then a lumpkin
Like me can do it, too.
(*She continues with determination.*)

(CLOWN *enters wearing an apron and carrying a broom. He puts an Inn sign near the bench and chair. He and* EXTREMELY LONG *come to life.*)

SMALL: Oh, an inn! (*Entering.*) Hi! Are you towns-folks?

INNKEEPER: We sure are.

SMALL: How do you do? My name is Small, and I'm from the country.

EXTREMELY LONG: Hello.

INNKEEPER: My name is Clown, and I'm the Inn-keeper.

SMALL: How do you do? And what's your name?

EXTREMELY LONG: My name is Extremely Long.

SMALL: Yes, but what is it?

EXTREMELY LONG: Extremely Long.

SMALL: Oh, how do you do, Mr. Long.

EXTREMELY LONG: How do you do?

INNKEEPER: Ah, what's that . . . Why are you wearing that . . . (*Points to pumpkin and nudges* EXTREMELY LONG.) You ask her.

EXTREMELY LONG: What my friend Clown wants to know is why is that peculiar orange fruit tied on your leg?

INNKEEPER: The pumpkin.

SMALL: You want to know what this pumpkin is doing on my leg? Well, that is really very simple. You see, I have never been to town before, and I was afraid that I might lose myself here among the new people. You know—not know who I was. So, I tied this pumpkin to my leg, and now, every time I look down and see the pumpkin, I know that it is me, Small. The person with the pumpkin is Small.

EXTREMELY LONG: I see.

INNKEEPER: Hmmmmmmm.

SMALL: Say, what do you townsfolks do for entertainment?

EXTREMELY LONG: Well, sometimes we tell funny stories. (*They laugh.*)

INNKEEPER: Sometimes we dance.

EXTREMELY LONG: And sometimes we sing a little.

MISHY, MASHY

Polka ♩ = 120

Mish - y mash - y, wish - y wash - y, ic - ke ock - le spoo.

How do you do? Cab - bage in your shoe. I

met a man who could -n't stand on one leg or on two. His

bones were made of knuc - kle meat; his feet were made of glue.

59

SMALL: Oh, I just love to sing and dance. If I sing a little song for you, would you dance with me?

EXTREMELY LONG: Certainly.

(SMALL Sings "Mishy Mashy" [page 59]. *This song works well as a polka.* SMALL *can sing to the first 16 measures and finish it out with a dance. Small picks up the pumpkin, still tied to her leg, and the three dance together, using the chair as the fourth person. They finish with* SMALL *and* EXTREMELY LONG *collapsing on the bench.*)

SMALL: Oh, that was fun, but I am tired!

EXTREMELY LONG: I am exhausted. I think I'll just go to sleep. (*The two nod out, leaning on each other.*)

INNKEEPER: Look at that! They both fell asleep. Well, if I want to get any sleep myself, I'd better clean up the place a little. (*He moves the chair aside and sweeps as far as* EXTREMELY LONG'S *crossed feet.*) These feet are in the way. (*He taps them with his broom.* EXTREMELY LONG *lifts them in his sleep;* CLOWN *sweeps under; the feet lower.* CLOWN *sweeps along, doing the same with each of* SMALL'S *feet. The pumpkin is next in line.*) Now the pumpkin is in the way. (*He knocks pumpkin; it doesn't move.*) Hey, move, pumpkin. I can't sweep with that here. (*He picks it up and tries to put it aside, but the rope stops him.*) I'll have to take it off for a minute.

(*He unties pumpkin, puts it on the chair, and finishes his sweeping. Starts to exit.*) Oh, I almost forgot. The pumpkin. I'll just tie it on again. (*He ties the pumpkin on* EXTREMELY LONG's *leg and exits.*)

SMALL (*stretches and gets up*): Oh, that was a good little nap. I better be getting home now, though. Clyde will be expecting me. (*She starts to leave.*)

Oh, where's my pumpkin? Oh, dear! Who am I? Where is Small? (*She sees pumpkin on* EXTREMELY LONG.) There you are, you silly thing. You gave me a fright. How did you get over there? (*Pausing to reflect.*) Let me see. The person with the pumpkin is Small, so that must be Small. (*She goes over to* EXTREMELY LONG *and shakes him.*) Come on, Small. Wake up. It's time to go home now. (EXTREMELY LONG *wakes, slightly annoyed.*) It's getting dark, and you know that you don't like the dark.

EXTREMELY LONG: I like the dark.

SMALL: No, you don't, Small. I know you don't.

EXTREMELY LONG: I'm not Small.

SMALL: You are, too. You are wearing the pumpkin, and the person with the pumpkin is Small.

EXTREMELY LONG: I am not Small. What is this pumpkin doing on my leg?

SMALL: You better hurry up and get home or Clyde will be worried.

EXTREMELY LONG: Clyde? I don't know any Clyde.

SMALL: Yes, you do. Clyde is your best friend. Come on home now. You promised to bring back that pumpkin so Clyde can make pie.

EXTREMELY LONG: I don't know what you're talking about. And I'm not going home with you.

SMALL: Oh, I don't know what to do. I'll have to get Clyde to help me. He'll make you come home. I just can't cope with this myself. *(She retraces the pattern of her walk in reverse.)*

EXTREMELY LONG: I don't want this silly orange fruit attached to my leg. I'll just take it off and tie it somewhere else. There, I'll tie it on this chair. *(He ties pumpkin to chair leg and exits.)*

SMALL *(arriving home)*: Clyde!

CLYDE *(coming to life)*: Hi! How was town?

SMALL: Oh, the most terrible thing has happened.

CLYDE: What?

SMALL: Small won't come home.

CLYDE: What do you mean, Small won't come home? Aren't you Small?

SMALL: Don't you remember? The person with the pumpkin is Small. And that person is back at the inn and won't come home.

CLYDE: Oh, dear. That's bad. What will we do?

SMALL: Would you please come with me and help me bring Small home? I can't do it by myself.

CLYDE: Of course, I'll help. Let's go back to town. Which way is the inn?

SMALL: Just follow me. (*They repeat the walk pattern to the Inn.*) Here's the inn, and there's the pumpkin. (*Pointing to chair.*) There's Small, see?

CLYDE (*walking around chair to study it*): Oh, Small. Boy, have you changed! What happened to you? Wow! Well, let's go home. We'll have pumpkin pie. (*Starts to leave and sees that chair doesn't follow.*) Small, aren't you going to come? You silly Small. Come on home. (*To* SMALL.) Say, you know, maybe this isn't Small. It certainly doesn't *look* like Small. Besides, if this is Small, then who are you?

SMALL (*worried*): I don't know.

CLYDE: I've got an idea. Would you like to be Small?

SMALL: Oh, yes, I always used to be Small.

CLYDE: Well, I think I can fix it. The person with the pumpkin is Small. Right?

SMALL: Right.

CLYDE: Well, then. (*Untying pumpkin from chair.*) I'll give you the pumpkin. (*Handing it to her.*) And now you're Small.

SMALL (*hugging pumpkin*): Oh, goody, goody. Now I'm me again!

CLYDE: Let's go home and have pumpkin pie.
(*They run home with pumpkin and exit with their chair as* CLOWN *enters and clears the bench, chair, and Inn sign.*)

BUILDING THE HOUSE

Characters:	Props:
TALL	4 large cardboard sides of
CLOWN	house with rope handles,
CLYDE	no windows or doors
SMALL	cut out
EXTREMELY LONG	1 cardboard roof with
	chimney
	4 cups
	a variety of cardboard
	hammers and saws
	1 real keyhole saw

(*Calliope music can play as the house is being built, fading out when the dialogue begins. The actors can move very quickly during the building, giving the feeling of a silent movie or animated toys. Spirits are very high throughout. Feel free to use your own way of bringing in and setting up the pieces.*

SMALL and CLYDE zip on carrying a side of the house. CLOWN and TALL appear from another side. CLOWN and CLYDE hammer the sides together; they can use real wooden pegs or tie little ropes at the corner while pretending to hammer. TALL and SMALL scoot out to bring in a third side. They hammer that in place while

CLOWN and CLYDE *hurry off to get the roof. All four carefully place the roof over the three standing sides and step back to admire it.* CLOWN *and* SMALL *go to get the front piece while* TALL *and* CLYDE *bring on four cups.* CLOWN *and* SMALL *see the cups and quickly set down the house front. Cups are passed out, and all give a fast toast to their accomplishment.* TALL *and* CLYDE *collect cups and take them inside house while* CLOWN

and SMALL *add the last piece. They struggle to get it fitted, turning it several different ways, ignoring the most obvious one until the end. They finally get it on, but* CLOWN *is on the outside. He knocks. They push the side open and whisk him in. All activity and music stop. Pause.*)

SMALL: It's awfully dark in here.

CLOWN: It is dark because there is no sunlight.

CLYDE: There's a lot of sunshine outside. Let's scoop some in through the chimney with our cups.

TALL: Good idea.
(*They reach through the chimney with cups to scoop in sunlight.* EXTREMELY LONG *enters, crossing stage, and walks around the house curiously.*)

CLYDE: It doesn't seem to be working.

EXTREMELY LONG: Is there someone in there? What are you doing?

CLOWN: We're scooping in sunshine with our cups. What do you think?

EXTREMELY LONG: You're scooping in sunshine with your cups. Why?

TALL: Because it's dark in here, of course.

EXTREMELY LONG: It's dark in there. Haven't you ever heard of a window?

ALL: A window?

EXTREMELY LONG: Sure. Everybody knows that a window is the best way of getting sunshine into a house! (CLYDE *saws a little window with keyhole saw in the front piece, while others brace the house. They take turns looking out, exclaiming.*)

CLYDE: Wow! Now I can look out.

TALL: I can't see very well.

SMALL: Let's make a bigger window so that we can all look out.

ALL: Yes. Yes. (CLYDE *saws a larger window. They exclaim.*)

TALL: Look at all the sunshine coming in.

CLYDE: Beautiful sunshine.

CLOWN: Let's make an even larger window by taking out the whole wall.

SMALL: Good idea. Clown. You're so smart. (*They knock it out and are delighted.*)

ALL: Sunny. Sunny. Wonderful!

TALL: If we removed the roof, I believe we could really have maximum sunlight. (*They knock it off.*) That is beautiful!

SMALL: Look at all that lovely sunshine.

CLYDE: It is really bright and wonderful.

CLOWN: This back wall is casting a little shadow. Let's take it off.

ALL: Definitely. (*They untie the ropes, if necessary, and knock it down.*)

TALL: And the side walls! (*The side walls float down with a tap.*)

CLOWN: Perfect.

CLYDE: Beautiful.

SMALL: This is the sunniest house I ever saw.

TALL: Exquisite sunlight.

ALL: (*They sing and dance inside the area of the house. You might add a verse of music without words, so characters can speedily clear the props lying about.*)

EENA, MEENA

(All run off. Or, if you do The Flagpole *next,* TALL *and* SMALL *stop* CLOWN *and* CLYDE *and indicate they must stay to do another job forgotten.* TALL *and* SMALL *exit together, leaving* CLOWN *and* CLYDE *leaning on each other.)*

THE FLAGPOLE

<table>
<tr><td>Characters:</td><td>Props:</td></tr>
<tr><td>CLOWN</td><td>None!</td></tr>
<tr><td>CLYDE</td><td></td></tr>
<tr><td>EXTREMELY LONG</td><td></td></tr>
</table>

(CLOWN, CLYDE, *and* EXTREMELY LONG *enter and form a three-person freeze. If this number follows House Building,* EXTREMELY LONG *joins the other two already there. They announce themselves.*)

CLOWN: Clown,

CLYDE: Clyde,

EXTREMELY LONG: and Extremely Long in . . .

ALL: *The Flagpole.*
(EXTREMELY LONG *exits, and the other two start pacing.*)

CLOWN: Do we have a problem. Oh, what a problem!

CLYDE: Boy, do we have a problem!

CLOWN: What are we going to do?

CLYDE: We have a problem! (*Pause.*) What's our problem?

CLOWN: What's our problem? Clyde, do you realize that tomorrow they are delivering a flagpole right here, and you and I have been elected to carry the flagpole from here (*indicating spot*) all the way to the town square (*moving across stage*) over here?

CLYDE: Oh, I don't want to do that. I wanted to go fishing tomorrow. And, besides, I've never even carried a flagpole in my whole life.

CLOWN: Do you think I've spent my whole life carrying flagpoles? I've never carried a flagpole either. I don't know the first thing about how to do it.

CLYDE: Well, we'd better think of something. Think, think, think. (*They pace.*) Oh, I know. We'll practice carrying a flagpole.

CLOWN: Wait a minute. Clyde, I've got an idea. *We'll practice* carrying a flagpole.

CLYDE: Yeh.

CLOWN: No, wait, we can't.

CLYDE: Why can't we?

CLOWN: We haven't got a flagpole to practice with. Because, if we had a flagpole, they wouldn't be delivering one tomorrow.

CLYDE: I never thought of that. Think, think, think.

CLOWN: What are we going to do?

CLYDE: Oh, I know. We've got to find something that *looks* like a flagpole and practice carrying that.

CLOWN: Wait a minute. We can find something that *looks* like a flagpole and practice carrying that.

CLYDE: Yeh.

CLOWN: Something tall . . .

CLYDE: . . . and thin . . .

CLOWN: And very majestic.

CLYDE: And something that looks down on everybody.
(EXTREMELY LONG *enters and rudely pushes through them.*)

CLOWN: What can we find?

EXTREMELY LONG: Pardon me. (*He exits.*)

CLOWN: Say—what about Extremely Long?

CLYDE: No, he'd never do it. He hates to do favors for people.

CLOWN: What does he like to do?

CLYDE: He only likes to do what *he* wants to do. What's his own idea.

CLOWN: Well, we could make him think it was his idea.

CLYDE: How could we make him think it is his idea?

CLOWN: We can flatter him.

CLYDE: What?

CLOWN: Flatter him. Say nice things about him.

CLYDE: Oh, it's very hard to say nice things about Extremely Long.

CLOWN: Well, we'll make them up. (EXTREMELY LONG *enters again and crosses stage*.) Extremely Long is very tall, don't you think, Clyde? (EXTREMELY LONG *overhears and stops to listen, pleased*.)

CLYDE: Oh, yes, and he is very nice and thin.

CLOWN: He's very majestic.

CLYDE: And he certainly does look down on everybody.

CLOWN: This is funny, Clyde, but you know, he reminds me of a flagpole.

CLYDE: A flagpole! (CLYDE *walks around* EXTREMELY LONG, *looking him over*.) Yes, you're right.

CLOWN: Clyde, speak of the very devil. Look who's here!

CLYDE: Why, look who's here.

CLOWN: Extremely Long! It is such a coincidence. Fancy meeting you here. We were just talking about you.

EXTREMELY LONG (*pleased*): Yes, I heard.

CLOWN: We were saying how very tall you are.

CLYDE: And how majestic, with your hair waving in the breeze.

CLOWN: Now this is very funny. Promise me you won't laugh, but Clyde and I were saying that you remind us of a flagpole. (*The three chuckle.*) But here's the really funny part. This is such a coincidence, in fact it is almost bizarre, because it just so happens that Clyde and I need a flagpole to practice carrying from there (*pointing out the two places on the stage*) over here to the town square.

EXTREMELY LONG: You need a flagpole.

CLOWN: That's right.

EXTREMELY LONG: I am available.

CLOWN: What?

EXTREMELY LONG: I would like to be a flagpole.

CLYDE: Oh, no, no, no. We wouldn't consider asking you.

EXTREMELY LONG: No, I'd like to be a flagpole—very much.

CLOWN: No, we couldn't.

EXTREMELY LONG: No, I'd really love to be a flagpole. You don't understand.

CLYDE: Beg us!

EXTREMELY LONG: Please, let me be a flagpole.

CLOWN: All right. You're a flagpole. Come on over here. (*They move to the delivery spot.*) You have just been delivered.

EXTREMELY LONG: All right, I have just been delivered. Wait. What color am I?

CLYDE: You are green, purple, and orange.

EXTREMELY LONG: Ugh.

CLOWN: What! Those are the colors of our beloved country! (*They snap to attention with a silly salute.*)

EXTREMELY LONG: Very well. I like it now.

CLOWN: Your flag is waving in the breeze. (EXTREMELY LONG *shakes his hair.*) Are you ready?

EXTREMELY LONG: Wait. What am I made of?

CLYDE (*knocking on his head*): Wood.

EXTREMELY LONG: I'm not hollow, am I?

CLOWN: No, no. Solid oak.

EXTREMELY LONG: Do I have a little gold ball on top?

79

CLYDE: It's an eagle. And it's flying.

EXTREMELY LONG: Ah. Will there be crowds waving?

CLOWN: Yes, yes. Are you ready now?

EXTREMELY LONG: Just a minute. I have to feel like a flagpole. (*He concentrates hard and then snaps up very stiffly.*)

CLOWN: Do you feel like a flagpole? (*He prods him.*) Yes, he does feel just like a flagpole. Okay, let's go. (EXTREMELY LONG *leans stiffly to one side and* CLOWN *grabs him around the shoulders, while* CLYDE *picks up his feet. There is much struggling, huffing, and groaning as they move across to the "town square."*)

CLYDE: I had no idea flagpoles were so heavy.

EXTREMELY LONG (*greatly enjoying himself*): Is my flag waving in the breeze?

CLOWN: Oh, yes. (*They set him down. He rocks back and forth until they balance him just right.*) There. Thank you. (CLOWN *and* CLYDE *move to one side.*) Oh, that was hard work!

CLYDE: I'm exhausted.

EXTREMELY LONG: I am a flagpole! It is wonderful.

CLOWN: My arms ache and my back aches.

EXTREMELY LONG: I love being a flagpole.

CLYDE: I don't think I can do that again tomorrow.

EXTREMELY LONG: Where are the crowds? I must find them. I want to show everybody how wonderful it is to be a flagpole. (*Exiting.*) Look, everybody. I'm a flagpole.

CLOWN: We've got to figure out a way to get out of carrying that flagpole tomorrow, Clyde, because, if that flagpole is anything like this one today . . . (*Sees the empty spot.*) Clyde.

CLYDE: What?

CLOWN: Where is the flagpole?

CLYDE (*seeing the pole's gone*): Wait a minute.

CLOWN: It was right here.

CLYDE: I know. (*They both run to look for it.*)

CLYDE (*spotting EXTREMELY LONG exiting*): Oh, there it is. It's walking away.

CLOWN: What?

CLYDE: I said, the flagpole is walking away.

CLOWN: Oh. Wait. What are we worrying about! If that flagpole can walk, why would we have to carry the one tomorrow?

CLYDE: What?

CLOWN: Listen. When they deliver the flagpole tomorrow, we won't have to carry it over to the town square. We can just let it walk by itself.

CLYDE: Of course! The flagpole can walk by itself, and we can go fishing!
(*They run off.*)

THE ROAD TO MARKET

Characters:	*Props:*
TALL	a bench
SMALL	a ground cloth (*about 6′ x 4′*)
CLOWN	a bag of real grain

(TALL, SMALL, *and* CLOWN *enter, spread the ground cloth, set the bench on it, form a pose, and announce themselves.*)

TALL: Tall,

SMALL: Small,

CLOWN: and Clown in . . .

ALL: *The Road to Market.*
(CLOWN *and* SMALL *exit.*)

TALL (*enjoying the day*): What a beautiful day! The sun is shining. The breeze is fragrant. I'm so happy to be here in front of my little house. It was a lovely idea to put out this bench and the indoor/outdoor carpeting. (SMALL *enters from one side, walking along intently. She passes* TALL.)

TALL: Oh, good morning! (*Floating around, picking imaginary flowers or such.*)

84

SMALL (*continuing on way*): Good morning.

TALL (*smelling the air*): La, la, la, la, la.

SMALL (*stopping*): Excuse me. What are you doing?

TALL: I am contemplating the beauties of nature: the warm sun, the fragrant air, the soft breeze, the . . .

SMALL: Don't let me disturb you. (*Continues on her way.*)

TALL: Pardon me, but why are you walking on the path in front of my house?

SMALL: I'm going to the town square.

TALL: The town square? The square is that way. (*Pointing.*) You're coming from there.

SMALL: Yes, but I'll be going there again in a little while.

TALL: Oh, I see. And, in the meantime?

SMALL: The farmers' market.

TALL: But . . .

SMALL: To buy chickens.

TALL: To buy chickens?

SMALL: Chickens.

TALL: How many?

SMALL: Six.

TALL: How will you be able to carry so many?

SMALL: I'll let them walk. I'll see you later. (*Starts to exit.*)

TALL: Ah, pardon me. When you and the chickens walk back to the town square, will you be coming this way or some other way?

SMALL: This way.

TALL: On this path in front of my house?

SMALL: Yes, on this path.

TALL: Please, no. I hate chickens. Don't bring them walking in front of my house.

SMALL: This is the way we'll be walking.

TALL: I am contemplating nature here by this path. I do not want noisy chickens running by messing up the path, ruining the air.

SMALL: We're going to walk right along here. It's the shortest way.

TALL: I won't allow it. I asked you politely no, and you won't listen to me. (*Raising voice.*) I'll chase them if you come here.

SMALL: Be careful. Your shouting will scare them.

TALL: Scare them? They're not even here. (*Stamps*

foot.) I'm just saying to you to not bring them by here.

SMALL: I tell you your shouting and stamping is scaring them. Now stop it.

TALL: I am not scaring them.

SMALL: There, look at that. They're running all over. (*She darts about to round up the imaginary chickens.*)

TALL: Would you stop that! They're running all over my path. You can't come this way. Shoo. Shoo. They're making a mess.

SMALL: Now *you're* making a mess. (*Tries to keep chickens from flying in the air.*) You just stepped on that egg she laid!

TALL: It had no right to lay an egg on my path. Get it out of here.

SMALL: All right. I'll just take this other egg and get it out of here. (*Throws egg over shoulder, and it accidentally "hits"* TALL.)

TALL: You just hit me with an egg, you fool. (*The struggle continues with running and darting around after the imaginary chickens, hitting the air and the ground with ad-lib exclamations. At the height of the fray,* CLOWN *enters doubled over with a heavy bag of grain. He walks through the middle of the fight and finally notices that something is amiss.*)

CLOWN: What is this! Stop. You almost made me spill my grain. (*They stop and look at him.*) What is going on?

SMALL: She won't let me pass with my chickens. She's scaring the daylights out of them.

TALL: I distinctly warned her not to bring those chickens on this path in front of my house.

CLOWN: Chickens?

SMALL: She has no right to chase them around like that. They're exhausted. Just look at them.

TALL: Will *you* just look at the mess instead! Feathers and dust everywhere. Broken eggs.

CLOWN: Chickens? Feathers? Eggs? You've lost your senses. Get a hold of yourselves. Look around you. What do you see? Nothing. There's absolutely nothing there.

SMALL (*taking his arm*): But, I was . . .

CLOWN: Don't jar me; you'll make me spill my grain. Nothing. Do you understand?

TALL: You don't understand.

CLOWN: I don't understand! Do you realize how foolish you both are? You say you have chickens here.

SMALL: Yes.

CLOWN: I'll show you how many chickens you have. Now look at this bag. (*He lowers it to the ground.*) Look inside. (*He opens it.*) It's full of grain. Right?

TALL: Right. It is full.

CLOWN (*empties the grain out onto ground cloth and proudly shows the bag*): Now what's inside?

SMALL: Nothing.

TALL: Nothing.

CLOWN: Right, nothing! Now put your chickens in it. (TALL *and* SMALL *run around catching the imaginary chickens and put them in the bag.*) Go on, get them all. Now look. (*He closes top and shakes bag.*) What is inside?

SMALL (*looking*): Nothing.

TALL (*looking*): There's nothing there.

CLOWN: Nothing! Right. (*Tapping their heads.*) Just like the insides of your heads. (*He walks past them, through the grain. Stops.*) Now think on that and improve yourselves. (*He steps into the bag and hops off.*) It's hardly safe to walk on the road anymore with such foolish people about.
(TALL *picks up bench and exits shaking her head.*)

SMALL (*calling*): Clyde, come help me with this. (CLYDE *runs on.*) I can take this grain home for the chickens.
(*They pick up the corners of the ground cloth full of grain and hurry off.*)

"WHEN I WAS A LITTLE CHILD"

This song could be used as a solo piece for any of your characters here or elsewhere. It might also be used at the opening, as an introduction to your characters, in which case you might want to create peppier music. Play around with it to see what feels right for your purposes.

Gently ♩ = 108

When I was a lit-tle child, I had but lit-tle
ev - er, ev-er shall, un - til the day I

wit; 'tis a long time a - go but I have no more yet. Nor
die, for the long - er I live the more fool - ish grow I. But

fool or fool-ish though I be, I sing my song quite hap-pi -

ly; when left a - lone to think and dream, on

things which are not what they seem, oh la - dee - da - dee -

doe, and la - dee-da-dee - day, it's time to go a - way.

STRETCH THE BENCH

Characters:

TALL
SMALL
CLOWN
EXTREMELY LONG

Props:

flat bench long enough for
4 people
4 hats

(TALL *and* SMALL *enter carrying a bench.*)

TALL: Where are we going to put this bench?

SMALL: I don't know, but we'd better find some place soon. It's getting heavy.

TALL: This is a good place right here.

SMALL: Good idea. We'll just put it down right here.

TALL (*sitting*): I'm ready for a rest. Whew! (*She takes off her hat, fans her face, and places hat on bench beside her.*)

SMALL (*sits, places hat on bench beside her, and wipes brow*): We won't be late, will we?

TALL: Oh, no, we can't be late. The bench is the meeting spot, and we've got the bench!

CLOWN (*hurrying on*): Oh, Tall, Small, there you are! I was afraid we'd have to call off the meeting. I couldn't find the bench anywhere.

TALL: It's right here.

CLOWN: Yes, I see. But it always takes forever to get to it.

SMALL: That's why we moved it.

CLOWN: Good idea. I'm not late, am I?

TALL: No, we just got here.

CLOWN: Good. Well, now that I'm here, guess I'll sit down. I'm exhausted from running around.

TALL: Please rest yourself. (CLOWN *walks around the bench looking for a place.* TALL's *and* SMALL's *hats each take up the space of a person.*)

CLOWN: Hmmm, there doesn't seem to be any room here, though. No room here either. There's no room on this bench.

SMALL: I have plenty of room.

TALL: So do I. (*She stands up, putting on her hat, and points to her spot.*) There's plenty of room right there.

CLOWN (*sitting*): Oh, of course. (*Putting his hat beside him on the bench.*) There's plenty of room. This is just fine.

TALL (*looking for a spot*): But there's no room for *me* now!

CLOWN: There isn't?

94

TALL: No.

SMALL (*putting on hat and getting up to look*): Well, *there,* why don't you sit in that spot? (*Points to hers.*)

TALL: Oh, of course! (*Sits and puts hat on bench.*) I didn't even see it.

SMALL: Wait, now there's no room for *me!*

TALL: Dear me.

CLOWN: Me, me, me. If we're going to solve this problem, we'll have to stop thinking about just ourselves and look for room for *all* of us.

SMALL: You're so smart, Clown. It's got to be here somewhere. (*They look around.*)

TALL (*pointing underneath the bench*): There's a lot of room under there.

CLOWN: Of course, lots of it. We'll just turn the bench over and there'll be room for all of us. (TALL *and* CLOWN *put on their hats, stand, and flip over the bench.*)

TALL (*sitting on one bench leg*): Oh, this is nice. (*Puts hat down on center of bench.*)

SMALL (*sitting on other bench leg*): Very good. (*She puts her hat down.*)

CLOWN: Wait a minute. Now there's no room under there.

TALL: Now this is silly.

SMALL: Where did it go?

TALL: This bench is just too small. If only we could stretch it or something.

CLOWN: I've got an idea! We'll just turn it over and stretch the bench, so we'll all fit. (*He puts hat on ground in front of bench and prepares for work.*)

SMALL: That's a marvelous idea. You're so smart. (*Gets up and puts hat on ground next to* CLOWN's.)

TALL: Let me put my hat here on the ground too so it doesn't get knocked off. (SMALL *and* CLOWN *turn over the bench.* TALL *puts her hat on ground next to the others and joins* SMALL *on her end.*) Stretch!
(*They begin pulling it and* EXTREMELY LONG *runs in late to the meeting.*)

EXTREMELY LONG (*running up*): What are you doing?

CLOWN: We're stretching the bench. Come on. Help. (EXTREMELY LONG *throws his hat down next to the others and joins* CLOWN. *He and* CLOWN *pull the group way over to one side.*) We're making it lopsided. (*They stop to survey.*)

TALL: There's too much manpower on your side.

EXTREMELY LONG: We'll just switch.

TALL: One, two, three, switch. (*All four cross over and begin stretching again. The same thing happens.*)

SMALL: That's not going to work either. (*They stop.*)

EXTREMELY LONG: We'll do it one more time. Ready, switch. (*This time after scrambling, they end with EXTREMELY LONG and SMALL on one side and TALL and CLOWN on the other.*)

TALL: Stretch! (*They pull evenly now.*)

SMALL: It's working!

TALL: Quick, sit on it before it snaps back. (SMALL *sits on one end,* CLOWN *on the other,* TALL *jumps next to* CLOWN, *and* EXTREMELY LONG *quickly zips into the last place.*)

ALL (*exclaiming happily*): We did it! (*Ad-lib.*) There's plenty of room. (*As they congratulate themselves,* EXTREMELY LONG'S *attention goes to the four hats on the ground in front of them and looks around worried.*)

EXTREMELY LONG: Just a minute here. There's something very wrong. Look at those hats. There are four of them. Right? One, two, three, four hats. But there are only . . . (*Counting everyone but himself.*) one, two, three people.

SMALL: Well, there's got to be another person around.

97

TALL: Of course. Look around for him. (*All look.*)

CLOWN: I don't see anybody.

SMALL: Let me count. (*She stands.*) Maybe you didn't do it right. There are one, two, three, four hats, and there are one, two, three people. (*Sits perplexed.*)

CLOWN: Three people!

EXTREMELY LONG: Four hats and three people.

TALL: Who could it be?

EXTREMELY LONG: There's an extra hat. Very strange.

CLOWN: Don't get upset. I'll figure it out. (*He gets up.*) Did everyone come with a hat? (*All nod.*) Was there a hat here when you came? (SMALL *and* TALL *shake heads.*) Then there's no problem. (*Walking by hats and people as he counts.*) There are one, two, three, four hats. And there are one, two, three . . . people. (*Sits defeated.*)

TALL: Three people.

SMALL: Spooks!

ALL: Oh, spooks! (*All hug each other in fear.*)

TALL: Now wait, this is just silly. We're doing something wrong. (*She jumps up and counts very quickly.*) There are one, two, three, four hats and one, two, three, three, three . . . (*Jumps into her place.*) There are only three people! (*All are excited and upset.*)

CLOWN: Now wait a minute. It's only an extra *hat.* Why let it ruin our day? I'll just pick it up and throw it away, and we won't even worry about it.

ALL (*ad-lib*): Of course. Throw it away. Just get rid of it. (CLOWN *picks up* EXTREMELY LONG'S *hat to toss.*)

99

EXTREMELY LONG: Oh, don't throw that hat away. That's my hat.

CLOWN: Oh, sorry.

EXTREMELY LONG: I'll take it. (CLOWN *hands it to him and picks up the next hat on the line.*)

TALL: Oh, don't throw that hat away. That's my little bonnet! (*She takes it and puts it on.*)

CLOWN: How about this one? (*Picking up the third in line.*)

SMALL: That's mine! (*She takes it and puts it on.*)

CLOWN (*picking up last hat*): All right, what about this one? Speak up.

ALL (*ad-lib*): It's not mine. I have mine on. Throw it away.

CLOWN (*stopping to look closely at both sides and sniffing inside*): Say, this is my hat! (*He puts it on.*) It's a good thing I spoke up in time. (*General exclamation.*)

TALL (*looking at ground where the hats used to be*): Say, there's no extra hat there.

EXTREMELY LONG: It's gone.

SMALL: This is spooky.

CLOWN: I don't like this spot.

EXTREMELY LONG: Let's pick the bench up and take it back to where it used to be.

(EXTREMELY LONG *and* CLOWN *pick up bench and quickly exit with it.*)

SMALL: Hey, wait a minute, guys!

TALL: We forgot to tell you why we called the meeting.

SMALL (*disappointed*): We wanted to sing a song for you!

TALL (*looking out at audience*): We could sing it for them.

SMALL: Yes, we'll sing it for you. Good idea.

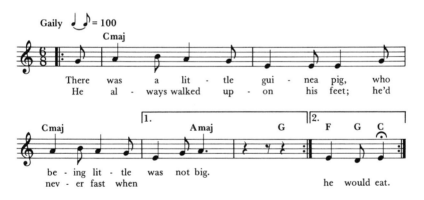

There was a lit - tle gui - nea pig, who
He al - ways walked up - on his feet; he'd

be - ing lit - tle was not big.
nev - er fast when he would eat.

When from a place he ran away,
He never at that place did stay.
And while he ran, as I am told,
He ne'er stood still
For young or old.

(*All exit.*)

MOON SHOT

Characters:	Props:
CLOWN	rocket ship (*large sheet of*
EXTREMELY LONG	*curved cardboard or fiber*
TALL	*barrel with doors cut out*)
SMALL	cardboard nose cone
CLYDE	cable (*or rope*) and "power
	box"
	cup

(*All walk out mesmerized, looking at a spot in the sky, and form a group freeze pointing up at it.*)

ALL (*looking forward*): *Moon Shot!*
(*They all march off,* CLYDE *to one side and the others to pick up the rocket ship equipment.*)

EXTREMELY LONG (*entering with cables and a "power box"*) : Right this way. Right this way. Don't drop anything. It's very valuable equipment.
(CLOWN *enters carrying front of ship;* TALL *is on the end.* SMALL *comes last wearing the nose cone.*) Careful now.

CLOWN: This is a very heavy rocket ship.

EXTREMELY LONG: Yes, this is the ship that is going to take us up to the moon.

CLOWN: This is the heaviest rocket ship I ever carried.

EXTREMELY LONG: To the moon, to find out if the moon is the same as the earth or if it is different from the earth or vice versa, if you catch my meaning.

TALL: Can we put it down?

EXTREMELY LONG: Yes, yes.

TALL: Where?

EXTREMELY LONG: The best place to put a rocket to the moon is . . . underneath the moon. Yes.

TALL: Good idea.

CLOWN: Where is the moon?

EXTREMELY LONG: I don't know. Where is the moon?

CLOWN: There it is!

EXTREMELY LONG: That's it. That means the ship has to go approximately right over there. A little more to the left. Ah, ah, over this way a bit. Perfect. And now the nose cone. (*They put the cone on top.*)

TALL: That is a pretty rocket ship.

SMALL: It looks beautiful!

CLOWN: It is the prettiest rocket ship I ever built.

EXTREMELY LONG: Splendid. You did an excellent job on the nose cone, Small. (*All shake each other's hands and ad-lib congratulations.*)

CLOWN: Say, if we want to send it up, we'd better do it pretty soon, because pretty soon it will be daytime, and there won't be any moon to go to.

EXTREMELY LONG: He's right.

TALL: We need fuel.

EXTREMELY LONG: Fuel.

CLOWN: Fuel.

SMALL: Fuel. (*The three scurry around and set up the cable and the power box.*)

EXTREMELY LONG: Get the fuel and be very careful with it. It is made of (*ad-lib content*), very high octane tomato juice and crispy cereal, and a dash of tabasco sauce and some pancake mix, and it's very explosive.

SMALL: I've got my part. Here you are. (*She gives* EXTREMELY LONG *the plug for power box.*)

CLOWN: We're getting ready. (*They set the power box of fuel behind the ship, wrap cable around ship, and hold plug far to one side.*)

EXTREMELY LONG (*taking one half of plug*): I need the right-hand section.

TALL (*giving him other half*): Here it is.

EXTREMELY LONG: Good. We're all ready to send it up.

CLOWN: Ready.

TALL: Wait, one minute. We forgot something. One of us has to go.

ALL: What?

EXTREMELY LONG: One of us has to get into the rocket to go to the moon. We need a volunteer.

ALL: Oh, I can't go.

EXTREMELY LONG: Why not?

TALL: I can't go because I'm your assistant, and I have to help you send it up.

EXTREMELY LONG: Oh, that's right.

CLOWN: Oh, oh, I'd love to go. I want to go. Oh, I really want to go.

EXTREMELY LONG: Good. A volunteer.

CLOWN: But I can't.

EXTREMELY LONG: Why not?

CLOWN: Because my mother won't let me cross the street by myself.

EXTREMELY LONG: Oh, Silly Soup. What are we going to do? I certainly can't go. I'm the director of the project, and directors never go any place.

SMALL: Well, I can't go.

ALL: Why not?

SMALL: Because I'm a scaredy cat, and scaredy cats can't go, that's why.

CLOWN: I've got an idea. We'll play a game, and the loser has to go.

TALL: Good, a game.

SMALL: I love games.

CLOWN: We'll all be very quiet and not say a word, and the first person to speak is the one who has to go to the moon. Agreed? (*He looks to* EXTREMELY LONG, *who nods yes, to* TALL, *who nods yes, and to* SMALL.)

SMALL (*nodding*): Agreed.

CLOWN: You're the one!

SMALL: Oh, no . . . ! You're sending *me* to the moon? (CLOWN *picks her up.* TALL *removes nose cone.*)

EXTREMELY LONG: Put her in the ship. (CLOWN *starts to lower her in head first.*)

SMALL: Hey, wait a minute, fellows. Can't you put me in a different way? This is killing me.

EXTREMELY LONG: Yes, put her in the front way.

CLOWN: In the front. Here we go. (*He sets her down;* TALL *opens the doors.* SMALL *steps in.*)

EXTREMELY LONG: We're ready to go. Batten the hatches. (CLOWN *and* TALL *close doors that hinge on front of rocket ship.*) Batten the hatches!

TALL: Hatches battened. (*She picks up nose cone to put into place.*)

SMALL: Just a minute! How will I get back from the moon?

EXTREMELY LONG: Ah, don't worry about a thing, Small. The moon people will know how to send you back.

CLOWN: That's right. They've lived there all their lives.

SMALL: All right.

EXTREMELY LONG: Good. Small, you're the first noodle astronaut. I wish you luck. Now remember to explore the moon and find out if it is the same as the earth or different from the earth. Then come back and tell us everything you have discovered.

CLOWN: Good-bye.

TALL: Good luck. (*Moves to put on nose cone.*)

SMALL: I'm going to the moon! Right? Me—to the moon. The moon! Ohhhh . . . (*She faints.*)

EXTREMELY LONG: We'll start the countdown.

CLOWN (*with fingers in ears and eyes closed*): Are you starting the countdown?

TALL: She fainted! (*Sets aside nose cone.*)

EXTREMELY LONG: She fainted?

CLOWN: Start the countdown.

EXTREMELY LONG: She fainted.

CLOWN: Okay, start the countdown.

EXTREMELY LONG (*pulling* CLOWN's *finger out of his ear*): She fainted!

CLOWN: Oh, don't start the countdown.

EXTREMELY LONG: Stop the countdown.

TALL: Get her some water.
(*They scramble around in confusion as* CLYDE *enters.*)

CLYDE: What's the matter?

EXTREMELY LONG: Get Small some water. (*Exits to look for some.*)

CLOWN: She fainted. (*Exits.*)

TALL: Water. (*Exits.*)

CLYDE (*looking in ship*): She fainted. I'd better get some water. (*He exits.*)
(SMALL *wakes up, sees she is alone, and is afraid. Outer space sound effects can be used here.*)

SMALL: Hey, where is everybody? Ohh . . . this is spooky. Where am I? I know: this must be the moon. I made it! (*Cautiously gets out of ship.*) I'm so proud of myself. I'm so brave. Now I must explore. Hey, you know, it's quite pretty here. There's ground and air and sky.

CLYDE (*entering with cup of water*): All right. Here's your water.

SMALL: Oh, help! A moon person! Stand back!

CLYDE: A moon person? (*Jumps back in confusion.*) Where?

SMALL: Yes, a moon person. Identify yourself. I am from the earth, and I am here on a moon mission. What are you doing here?

CLYDE: I brought you some water. (*Hands her the cup.*)

SMALL: Oh, thank you very much. (*Drinks.*) Very nice. Isn't this a coincidence! They have cups of water here, too, just like back home. (*Putting cup into ship.*) I think I'll keep this.

CLYDE: Back home? (*Giggles.*)

SMALL: Would you mind doing that again? (CLYDE *repeats.*) That sounds very familiar. You remind me very much of someone I know back home.

CLYDE: Who?

SMALL: My best friend, Clyde.

CLYDE: Well, I'm a friend, and my name is Clyde.

SMALL: Isn't that a coincidence!

CLYDE: Are you sure you feel all right?

SMALL: I feel fine. Though, now that you mention it, I do feel a little lightheaded. Like weightless. They told me that might happen. (*She starts a slow motion walk.*)

CLYDE (*To himself*): That must be because she fainted. (*To* SMALL.) That looks like fun. Can I try? (*He follows her.*)

SMALL: Sure. It *is* fun. It feels like being in a dream. Let's dance.

CLYDE: I'm not very good at it.

SMALL: Well, give it a whirl anyway. (*They do a weightless dance, giggling throughout.*) Push me. (*He does, and she returns it.*) Push me harder. (*Same, but as he turns, he falls before she can catch him. Moon music stops.*) Oh, you fell down. Did you get hurt? Oh, I wouldn't want anything to happen to you.

CLYDE: No. I'm okay.

SMALL: You're awfully nice. You're not at all spooky, the way I thought moon people would be. Would you mind showing me about the place? I am supposed to explore.

CLYDE: Show you around? Well, this is This Place.

SMALL: This Place.

CLYDE: Like it?

SMALL: I love it, really. Beautiful.

CLYDE (*crosses to other side*): And that's That Place.

SMALL: That Place.

CLYDE: How do you like that?

SMALL: This and That. Oh, fabulous.

CLYDE: And that's Back (*Pointing*) and that's . . .

SMALL: Wait. I bet I know. Front?

112

CLYDE: Yes, and that's Up (*Pointing down*) and that is . . . no, (*Switches*) that's Up (*Pointing up*) and that's Down.

SMALL: What do you know! We've got all this back home. This, That, These, Those, our Ups and Downs. Everything like here. Well, guess I'm ready to go now.

CLYDE: Are you really going to go in the rocket ship to the moon?

SMALL: The moon? You mean the earth.

CLYDE: No, I mean the moon . . . I think.

SMALL: Oh, I get it. These moon people here must call the earth the moon and the moon the earth? (*Looking at sky*). Well, you know, now that I look at it, the earth does look a little bit like the moon, doesn't it? Well, thank you very much. You have been most helpful.

CLYDE: Climb into the rocket ship, and I'll batten the hatches. (*The others re-enter;* SMALL *sees them and waves just as* CLYDE *puts on the nose cone.*)

CLOWN: I couldn't find any water. Do you have water?

EXTREMELY LONG: No water. I couldn't find any.

TALL: No water anywhere.

CLYDE: That's okay. I gave her some water. She's all ready to go.

CLOWN: Good.

EXTREMELY LONG: All right. Let's start the count-down. Everyone help. Ready? Ten.

ALL: Nine.

ALL: Eight.

ALL: Seven.

ALL: Six.

ALL: Five.

ALL: Four.

ALL: Three.

ALL: Two.

ALL: One.

ALL: Zero!
(*He connects plug. Lights flash and there is a blastoff sound.*)

CLOWN: There it goes! (*They all run to a spot.*)

EXTREMELY LONG: There it is.

CLOWN: No, that's a bird.

EXTREMELY LONG: Yes, that's a bird.

CLOWN: A-okay. Over and out! There it is. (*All run over.*)

EXTREMELY LONG: No, no.

CLOWN: That's a dirigible.

EXTREMELY LONG: A dirigible.

CLOWN: Oh, oh, there it is. (*He is looking up, hitting nose cone.*)

TALL: Where? Where?

CLYDE: There it is. There it is.

CLOWN: Fellows. Fellows. Look. (*Points to ship.*)

ALL: Oh . . . h . . . h . . .

EXTREMELY LONG: It didn't go anywhere. It didn't go up.

CLYDE: Small is going to be very disappointed. I don't want to be the one to have to tell her.

TALL (*to* EXTREMELY LONG): You'll have to tell her. You're the director.
(SMALL *pops out very excited.*)

SMALL: Hi, fellows; I'm back! Oh, was I a success! Just wait until you hear about it.

CLOWN: Small . . . Small.

EXTREMELY LONG: Small . . .

SMALL: What's the matter?

EXTREMELY LONG: Small, I'm very sorry to tell you, but the rocket was a flop.

SMALL: Oh, no it wasn't!

EXTREMELY LONG: You didn't go anywhere.

SMALL: Oh, yes I did.

CLOWN: It didn't go up.

SMALL: I went to the moon. I'm the first female astronaut. At first it was very spooky, but . . .

EXTREMELY LONG: You didn't go anywhere. You were here all the time.

SMALL: . . . but then I started to look around. . . .

CLOWN: Small, you couldn't have gone. We never saw you leave; we were here all the time.

EXTREMELY LONG: We were here all the time.

CLOWN: No, wait a minute. We weren't here *all* the time. Remember she fainted, and we went to get her a drink of water?

TALL: Maybe she did go to the moon!

SMALL: Of course, I went! They had This, That, These, Those, their Ups and Downs.

EXTREMELY LONG: Maybe she went while we were gone.

SMALL: Of course. I told you, when I first got there it was spooky, but, when I looked around, it was really pretty. Then I saw my first moon person. It was somebody who looked very much like Clyde. (*She hugs him.*)

OTHERS: Hey, Small, Small, Small.

CLOWN: Did you see someone who looked very much like me?

EXTREMELY LONG: Did you see somebody who looked very much like me?

TALL: Did you see somebody who looked very much like me?

SMALL: Just before I left, I saw someone who looked just like you and you and you.

EXTREMELY LONG: Oh, wonderful! The moon must be a great place if there is someone there who looks like me.

CLYDE: Boy, people everywhere must be exactly like us!

CLOWN: Small, was everything on the moon just like here on the earth?

SMALL: Everything was very much the same. Only one thing was different.

EXTREMELY LONG: What was that?

SMALL: On the moon, you walk funny, like this. (*Demonstrates.*)

EXTREMELY LONG: Oh, that's . . . that's weightlessness. It's a phenomenon.

CLYDE: It's a funnynomenon. (*They all start to try it.*)

CLOWN: It's a moon phenomenon. Oh, I'd love to be weightless.

CLYDE: This is fun. (*All do weightless walk.*)

EXTREMELY LONG: I'd like to go to the moon.

CLOWN: Me, too.

CLYDE: I want to go, too.

TALL: Let's go. Let's go, too.

CLOWN: I have an idea. Let's throw away this little, tiny rocket ship, and build a great big one . . .

EXTREMELY LONG: Yes . . .

CLOWN: And we'll all go to the moon!

ALL: To the moon! (*Pick up ship and run off.*)

(If this is the last piece on your program, all could pop out again and sing a reprise of the opening song and/or do a dance.)

GETTING YOUR SCENE TOGETHER

Funny situations have so many delightful angles that it's not possible to say exactly what works to get us laughing. Sometimes wonderful things happen that none of us is smart enough to explain. There are several things that we know usually work to make people laugh. They're given here as a guide and a checklist to help you get on the right track. You'll know very well, however, when you look at the scene whether or not it's funny. Intuition is usually a good guide. The things written here are to help you trust what your intuition is probably already telling you. There are other points we're more sure about which help you play any scene in a way that holds it together and makes sense to an audience. We'll talk about those things first.

To get started with the scripts, pick one you want to try and read it through aloud. Decide who's going to play the different parts and read it aloud again. You don't have to do this, of course, but it's a way to become familiar with the situation, the progression of ideas, the action, the attitude of the characters and their way of behaving. Then you can put the script aside and act out the scenes, improvising your own words. Follow the action of the plot or develop your own variations. Let the characters respond to the situation in their own fashion. In fact, you might want to try starting with only the beginning situation and let the characters come up with completely new solutions.

When you're acting out a scene, be clear about who is in it, where the action takes place, and what the characters are doing. What they are doing has two parts: one is the overall problem they're trying to solve (for example, delivering the gold or building a house) and the other is the activities they do to solve the problem (such as carrying the heavy bag or cutting a window). As long as you're clear about these things, you won't have trouble developing your scenes, whether you stick closely to the script, use just the plot line from the script, use only the opening situation, or even work from other stories that you've read or heard or made up.

A scene, by the way, is a division of a play. It concerns action occurring in one physical place and is usually about one idea. A simple play may have only one scene. Many of those in this collection are like that. More complicated plays introduce several ideas and often several locations. When there are many scenes, they are often grouped into acts; then two or more acts make up the play. None of these plays, however, is that involved.

Whether your play has one scene or many, check to see that it has a beginning, a middle, and an end. If you're using a script, the playwright has designed those parts for you; identify them when you use the script. If you improvise your play from a situation, a plot, or a story, you need to set them up. In the beginning we introduce the main characters, their situation, and something that changes their situation to get the action rolling. In the middle we see the characters dealing with the issue at hand. In the end we see the main character or characters make a final decision which will settle the question or problem.

At any point in your rehearsing you could return to the script and re-read it to check how a particular idea was developed there and what dialogue those characters use. The sequence and timing of the exchanges in the scripts were carefully worked out. Looking at it again might help you rework your own ideas. Your final acted version of the plays might combine the scripts and your own ideas.

CREATING COMIC CHARACTERS

In making characters for zany plays, you will want to create people so whimsical and wacky you'd never expect to meet them in real life. You see *parts* of them everywhere, because comic characters are exaggerations of real people. One or two traits of a person are singled out and presented as the whole person. So that we can clearly see those traits you've selected, keep the characters very simple. It's usually more effective if the boaster is always boastful and never modest, if the slow plodder never jumps into fast action. The characters need to be single-minded and intense. Their one-sidedness makes them ridiculous and funny. Look around for a part or two of a real person that would be fun to work with. Check yourself, other people, even animals. Is there a particular thing that any of them does that strikes you as funny? Could it be the way you find you are holding your body when you're asking someone for a special favor? Or the way your teacher uses his voice when he gives directions, or your dog tenses her face when scratching fleas? Borrow it and try it on to see what it does for you. Let it take over and become your total self.

Gestures could be a starting point. Try one that you've noticed someone using and let yourself take on the attitude behind it. For instance, suppose you decide to try throwing up your hands whenever your character has expressed an opinion. As you do this, you'll find you get some insight into how your character feels. Allow that feeling to develop. You might find the character is using the gesture to say, in effect, "I'm not responsible for what I say," or perhaps you discover it is a proud movement, meaning, "How about that idea!"

Words can suggest a type of person to you, too: dreamer, rigid, vain, cautious. Look at photographs, drawings, sculpture, cartoons for more ideas; there the artist has already made some selections to point out to you. Any of these could give you a good start for the creation of your character.

Experiment with physical changes. Exaggerate yourself into being very large or very small. Try being crooked. Move very loosely or very stiffly. Changes in your shape can come through the way you use your body or through costumes you wear. Try padding your clothing or wearing things like tall hats, big shoes, or tight pants. When you take on an unusual body shape, see what happens to the way you behave. This new behavior can create the character for you.

Another kind of physical change could be a rhythm change. What person appears when you move in a very uneven rhythm? What happens if you do everything more quickly or more slowly than normal? For a real challenge, see if you could work with unexpected combinations, such as a tiny voice in a large body or slow movement with fast talking.

People's ways of holding and using their bodies are clues to their feelings about themselves and the world. You discover these feelings or attitudes when you work with the physical changes. But you can also go about it the other way and start with the feelings. Suppose you walk around with the attitude, "Why does it always have to happen to me?" What happens to your body when you feel this way? How would your body change if you moved around feeling, "No one here begins to measure up to me!"? And what happens to your movement if your character always feels, "This is the most exciting place I could possibly be!"?

Once you've started creating your character, a way to get to know him better is to give him a small job to do, such as putting on a jacket or moving a chair to just the right spot. Let a problem develop so he'll have to spend more time playing with it. Be very open to letting the character move in her own way, not your customary way. From such simple tasks, you can often discover how she would behave in the other, more complicated situations of the play. Every time the character is on stage, you need to make clear what he/she is doing, and why, and how he/she feels about it.

As you get a sense of who this person is, one aspect will affect another, until you've discovered the right voice, body, and feelings for your character. It doesn't matter which part you pick as your starting point as long as you end up with both an attitude and a physical self. A character with only physical qualities would be too uninteresting and shallow. A character with only an attitude couldn't work because it is the character's body and voice that show us how he or she is feeling. When you create characters in this open way, you'll often be as surprised as anyone by the person that appears. This person is separate from you with a life of its own, and it is also part of you because it came from you. Whatever choices you make along the way, part of yourself always needs to be there to bring the character to life. This is true both when you are originally creating the character and when you re-create it in each performance. The more fully you behave as that character, the more fun you'll have with it. You are the energy and the life; the character is the form you fill with life. That's the fun and the art of acting.

HOW FUNNY IS FUNNY?

When you read these plays or act them out with your friends, have fun with them in your own way. They are here for your enjoyment. If you decide you also want to share your playing with an audience, there are a few things to consider which will help you create a good time for everyone. One is the overall tone of humor in your acting. The situations in these plays, and the way the characters respond to them, are absurd and ridiculous. But the plays don't ridicule or make fun of the characters. The fun is in our laughing *together* rather than laughing *at someone*. It feels like fun because the plays are really about us —our own craziness. To make fun of someone or something is not the same thing; we all know what it feels like to be the one laughed at: no fun. If you keep love and acceptance in the craziness you create with these characters, the fun and funniness will have a happy feeling.

Within this tone, you can play the scenes in any style of comedy you like best: a broad, burlesque way or a gentle, low-key manner, or anywhere in between. You often see very broad humor on television. It is loud and fast and usually rough or even violent. The characters yell at each other a lot and hit and fall down. Often they play their reactions straight out to the audience. Sometimes this is very funny. Sometimes it's just noisy. If you work in a broad, slapstick style, make sure you do things that you think are really funny. It helps if you think of making the action large, clean, and physical. If you're just carried away with the noise and running around, the action will become very tiring for the audience. Also be careful not to let the characters become nasty to each other; this would work against your feeling of good humor.

In gentler kinds of humor, characters are still exaggerations of real life, but all their responses are more contained. The characters create a world of their own and live in it, concerned mainly with each other rather than with outside watchers. Some comedy that is truly amusing and involving for the audience brings about little smiles rather than outright laughs. The whole situation can be charming rather than outrageous.

Whatever your style, the world you create for your characters needs to be the same world for all of them. It's confusing to have some characters behaving in a broad, loud style and others in a gentle low-key manner. Find the way that best fits most of the characters you've created; then let their range of differences stay within that world.

In making your choice you may also want to think about who your audience will be. It's pretty easy to judge what your own tight circle of friends will enjoy, but the special sense of humor of your own group isn't always appreciated by people outside it. If your audience is a larger group, you'll need to widen the appeal. Are they going to be the neighbor-hood kids, the first-grade class, your families? Each will respond a little differently. It's not necessary to go into a whole study about it; just take a few minutes to imagine what they'd appreciate. You might even invite a few people from your expected audience to watch a rehearsal, so you can see their reactions.

When you're sharing your plays with an audience, have a good time yourself! Sometimes, when people perform comedies, they work so hard to get the other people laughing that they stop having fun themselves. At the other extreme, sometimes they laugh so much at their own jokes that they never create a full scene for the audience to enjoy. It isn't hard to avoid these problems if you enjoy the acting as much when you do it for others as when you do it for yourself and if you express your enjoyment by playing your character with lots of energy and full concentration.

SHAPING THE PIECE

When you practice your play, the early rehearsals are for exploring, for trying lots of different ways. In later rehearsals, after you've made choices about things to keep and things to drop, you begin to shape the scenes and fit them together as a whole. This section is about the fine points of shaping. If it seems too complicated for your interest, skip on to the next.

Any comedy scene is helped by economy, no matter what your style or for whom you're playing. Cut out extra, unnecessary action and lapses between action or words. Some pauses and stops are necessary; don't rush through or cut out those. Silence is as important as sound, stillness as important as movement. Select just what you need of each and then balance it. Fewer, well-done exchanges are always more effective than many actions that become blurred.

Pacing of scenes in comedy is also important. The pace or tempo means how fast or slow you play something. Usually things work better in comedies when they are faster than in real life. Being economical is one way of picking up the pace. Simply moving and talking more quickly is another. If you go faster, though, be sure you still do everything fully and clearly! It's a real challenge.

Within the pace you've set, pay attention to the rhythm. If everything moved at one speed, without different rhythms, the scene would be monotonous and hard to follow. You need fast and slow sections, pauses, highs and lows of pitch and intensity. Something that will help you with the rhythm is being aware of the way a scene is made up of beats. Beats are small units of action within a scene focusing on a particular idea. For instance, in *Bag of Gold*, when Clown and Clyde are working out a trade with the innkeeper, it is one beat from the time they say they want to do business with her until they agree upon the paper bags. The next beat starts right away as Clyde begins to doubt their success and ends where he convinces Clown they've been cheated. Keep the flow of exchange between the characters going from the beginning until the end of the beat so that the action of that unit stays in focus. There can be variations of rhythm and tempo within a beat, but treat the total rhythm of a beat as a unit. Working this way makes the ideas in your piece easier to understand.

Certainly in everyday life we use rhythms to make our meaning clear. Try talking in an even-pace-monotone-pitch-no-emphasis voice. It feels weird because it's very unnatural; it's also very difficult to understand. It would be equally confusing if you and a friend discussed two different topics and had no pauses or changes in rhythm as you shifted from one idea to the next.

Another element to consider is timing. This is the subtlest division of shaping. It is the exact way in which you control the pace and rhythm of your playing. In comedy, you know that a joke won't work when the punch line is rushed or comes too late. You sense it and know when the moment is just right. Timing is part of both comic and serious acting. The more you're aware of it, the more fun you can have playing with it.

Pace, rhythm, beats, and timing are all theater terms as well as musical terms. That's no accident. In theater the actor or player also plays an instrument; it is his or her body. The "music" is the action of the character, the sound and movement the character makes.

If you find in shaping your piece that you don't like parts of it, step back from it to think about some of the suggestions in this section. Making things funny is tricky because the number of times you do something and the intensity with which you do it make a big difference in the effect. A physical exaggeration in a character could easily become gross instead of funny. Or an unexpected turn of events might be scary instead of funny.

When you're doing a scene for the players' fun of it, your best guide as to whether or not something is working is how it feels to all of you. If you're also going to share your scenes with an audience, you need to check to see if it feels right to the people watching as well. Take turns being audience for each other. Ask friends outside your group to watch. Have them tell you what they liked and why, and what they didn't like and why. Make sure they are telling you how they reacted and not what they think you should have done. If there are parts of your scene that made them feel uncomfortable or bored, and if these parts don't feel right to you either, see if any of the following questions give you clues about what changes to make.

Does the scene have something new, fresh, unexpected? Are there contrasts, such as large and small, fast and slow, best and worst, hoped for and actual? Are there exaggerated physical changes in your characters? Are the characters single-minded, simple-minded, unaware of themselves, fully concentrated? When they struggle to solve their problems, are they likable in their wackiness or have they become scary or annoying or boring or pathetic? Is your scene hard to see or hard to hear? Are the separate ideas made clear? Is the pace a little too slow or a little too rushed? Do you have variety in the speed, in the movement, in the use of the playing area?

If none of these pointers helps, try a variety of very large changes, such as playing the whole scene with huge movement and no words, or doing it with small tight movement and super fast speech. Going through several such different approaches is usually a funny challenge for the actors and often it jogs all of you into seeing new possibilities for your final solution.

SONGS AND MUSIC

The songs given here are for you to pick from and use in a way that feels comfortable to you. If music seems like a problem, don't use any at all. The scenes that have songs written into them can work with other action substituted. For instance, in *Pumpkin,* Small could recite her poem at the inn instead of singing a song, and she and the "townsfolk" could play vigorous jumping or chasing games together instead of dancing.

Songs are a lively addition that are fun, however. You needn't shy away from them just because you think your voices aren't very good. Who would ever expect a noodle to be a great singer? (Except herself, of course.) And you needn't give up on songs because no one of your group can play musical accompaniment. Sing unaccompanied. Or accompany with a little rhythm band of percussion sounds. You could get someone who plays an instrument to help you by playing once while you record it on tape; then have someone from your group operate a tape recorder to provide the music when you rehearse and perform. Of course, if anyone in your group can and wants to play a melodic instrument, you could use live music. It could be provided by one musician or a little orchestra sitting to one side of your stage area, or by an actor who becomes a musical character and plays as part of the action.

The music given with the songs shows the melody line alone. Expand on these melodies in any way you'd like: add harmonies, change keys, try the guitar chords shown above the notes, use as many musical voices as you'd like. You may want to try making up your own melodies as well. You could make up a rhythm pattern and sing-speak the words of one of the songs or you could adapt one of your melodies to this rhythm. There may be places in the play where you will want to add a whole new song for one or more of the characters. Let the words come out of the dramatic situation and express the feeling the character has at that time. Those feelings could be his or her specific reaction to what is going on or just an outburst of crazy energy. In addition to songs there could be background music: circus-type music for tricks or action without words, outer space music for Small's moon walk. Sound effects are fun to add, especially when you're doing things like opening and closing imaginary doors. What about a rocket blast-off? Use as much or as little of this sound and music as you like.

The music or the songs could be treated as separate numbers, as part of a scene, or as a bridge between scenes. Turn any of the songs or pieces of music into a dance if you want. A song or a dance is a lively means to get all of your company into action together. It makes a sparky introduction and ending to a presentation if you are sharing your plays with an audience.

PRODUCTION NOTES

WHERE TO DO THE PLAYS

Your playing area needs to be big enough for your actors to move freely but small enough that they don't get lost in it. It can be in a variety of places. Stages in school auditoriums are often difficult places in which to perform. Think about using an open space in an all-purpose room, classroom, living room, or outdoors. If you have an audience, of course, their space needs to be big enough to hold them comfortably. If there're enough people so that they have to sit one behind the other, either they or the actors will need to be raised, or people will have a hard time seeing and hearing. Keep the distance between actors and audience close enough that you won't have to strain your voices to be heard. If audience size becomes a problem, do more than one performance for smaller groups.

A playing area can be in a variety of shapes. The actors can play at one end of the space and face the whole audience. Or the audience can sit in a half-circle around the playing area, or three-quarters around it, or form a full circle with the stage in the center. Actors can even move through the audience or have several playing areas throughout the whole space. It's a bit easier to perform comic scenes if the audience sits opposite the actors or in a half-circle because the humor in a situation sometimes depends upon all the audience seeing an action happen at the same time. With a little extra practice, however, you can be equally effective in any set-up of stage to audience. Remember to share the action of your characters with all viewers. Face out or open up your action to be seen from as many different directions as possible. Move to different edges of your playing area so the same actors aren't always in front of the same section of audience. Avoid standing shoulder to shoulder, thereby forming a wall difficult to see through. Practice having those on stage throw the focus of the scene to the characters you want the audience to be watching at a particular time.

Whatever the size or shape of your playing area, use all parts of it fully. Notice if there are areas never used or others overused. Can you change the placement of chairs, benches, doors, entrances, or exits to help the characters use the whole space in a more interesting and natural way? Remember that, above all, you are sharing something with your audience. Take turns watching from the various places where people would be sitting to see if your actors are playing the scenes in a way that is open to everyone.

SCENERY

The scenery for these plays can be extremely simple. The plays aren't about real places; it's better if the settings they represent are as oversimplified and unreal in visual design as they are in the situations. A sign declares an inn. A chair is home. A knock on an imaginary door with an accompanying sound effect will put it there without anything having to be built. Another reason for using abbreviated scenery is that the action zips in and out of places quickly. A lot of fun would be lost by slowing down the action to bring in scenery each time the location changed.

One useful item of scenery would be some kind of a backdrop or screen behind which the characters can disappear and reappear as the scene requires. Props could also be hidden there until they're needed. Or put props in a chest on one side of the stage for actors to go to when they need an object for the scene. A bench, chairs, or stools are used in a number of scenes. These shouldn't be hard to find. If you choose to do the plays calling for the house or rocket ship, you can have fun making these things out of cardboard. As long as they stand up and aren't too cumbersome for the characters to handle, they can look as crazy as you want to make them. (You can even make these things out of other actors—or out of thin air!) If you feel that making an actual rocket ship is too complicated, you haven't gotten far enough into the noodle way of thinking!

PROPS

Props or properties are the things the actor uses in the play that are small enough to be carried in hand. There are a number of props in these plays. You could gather real objects (hammers, cups) or fake objects (gold bricks, fuel box for rocket) or make everything flat cardboard cutouts. You might think of making all the things larger or smaller than normal. You could paint them in bright colors or crazy designs. Because there's so little scenery, props can be the means for having visual fun. If you're presenting the plays to an audience, give the things you use the kind of unity you give your acting, so the objects will look as though they belong to the same world.

Props can be funny in themselves, but remember that objects gain their real humor from the way the actors use them. Give yourself plenty of experimenting and practicing time to work with any objects you're going to use. You want them to be a help to the show instead of a bother to the actors!

COSTUMES

The costumes can be as simple as the scenery. They might be fairly normal or rather wacky. If you do put together crazy-looking outfits, don't forget that the characters take themselves seriously. Just as they are variations of normal people, their clothes are also variations of the normal.

An easy way to unify your group is to dress everyone in the same basic outfit, such as overalls or jeans, and then use different tops. A variety of hats is fun and effective in distinguishing one character from another. All characters could, of course, be in different outfits, as people would be in real life. If you want each completely different, pick the kind of clothes and the color that seem to best fit the personality of each character. You could also use costumes to affect the size of your people or to emphasize a physical quality: long skinny lines; wide padded forms; loose, floppy layers.

When you've gathered the clothing you want to use, have a look at everything together and see if the costumes help emphasize the personalities of the various characters and give the impression that these people are living in the same world. You may need to make some changes to create a good balance between individual variation and overall unity. If you want more detailed help on making costumes, props, or scenery, consult some of the books described in the bibliography in the back of this book.

BEING FUNNY ISN'T EVERYTHING

A final word about sharing these scenes with an audience: being funny isn't the only goal. You might turn yourself inside out trying for laughs and end up with a few of them and nothing else. Remember, a comedy can be wonderful fun and hold our interest without making us laugh out loud.

These plays and the original stories they are based on are funny because they invite us to look at the world in a different way than we normally do. It's fun to watch characters who totally ignore basic things we know to be true. We know better than these noodles, of course, but because they are so intent about everything they do and are so completely delighted with their ridiculous solutions, we take joy in watching them. We can love them for letting us see the everyday world through their eyes.

AUTHOR'S NOTE

Two of the things I most loved about working with noodlehead stories were, first, being tripped up again and again by their wonderful world view and then discovering that world view (and even some of the same plot lines) popping up in tales from very distant parts of the world.

The Wise Men of Chelm built the largest, most beautiful synagogue they could raise and were delighted until they noticed how dark it was inside. No windows to let in sunshine! Undaunted, they selflessly volunteered to carry in the sunshine to finish the job. All pitched in, helping with buckets, pitchers, and wheelbarrows, and who knows but what they're still at it. That might not be so strange, but according to the Gotham tale, their like-minded English cousins had the same problem with their brand-new cathedral!

Jogging is my updated version of an ancient Chinese story—or so my source indicated. But at the close of one performance an elderly couple came up to thank us for "that Sholem Aleichem tale of the wrong shoes."

Have the tales traveled or is foolishness universal? Either theory pleases my sense of world brother/sisterhood.

At any rate, folks hear tales and adapt them just as we did with the Chelm story of carrying freshly cut trees back up the hill in order to let them roll down because everyone had been too foolish to see this easy solution on the first trip. We had no trees; we had no hill. So we practiced carrying a flagpole from this place to that, but we wisely dropped the project when we realized the pole could have walked by itself anyway.

You'll be able to find noodlehead tales in almost any library. I've listed my favorite sources in the bibliography. Two additional ones, wonderfully old books, are W. A. Clouston's *The Book of Noodles: Stories of Simpletons, or Fools and Their Follies* (London: Elliot Stock, 1903) and *The Merry Tales of the Mad Men of Gotham*, edited by A. B. Phisicke, reprinted from the rare original of 1630 by W. C. Hazlitt (London: Willis & Sotheran, 1866).

I hope you'll have as much fun with noodlehead humor as I have had.

BIBLIOGRAPHY

NOODLEHEAD TALES

The books recommended here focus on tales from the Gotham and Chelm traditions. Noodlehead tales also appear, however, in folk literature of other cultures.

Jagendorf, M. A., *The Merry Men of Gotham*. New York: Vanguard Press, 1950.

——, *Noodlehead Stories from Around the World*. New York: Vanguard Press, 1957.

Leach, Maria, *Noodles, Nitwits, and Numskulls*. New York: World Publishing Co., 1961.

Singer, Isaac Bashevis, *The Fools of Chelm and Their History*. New York: Farrar, Straus, and Giroux, 1973.

——, *When Shlemiel Went to Warsaw and Other Stories*. New York: Farrar, Straus, and Giroux, 1968.

Solomon, Simon, *The Wise Men of Helm*. New York: Behrman House Publishers, 1959.

Tenebaum, Samuel, *The Wise Men of Chelm*. New York: Thomas Yoseloff, 1965.

ACTING FOR CHILDREN

Edelson, Edward, *Funny Men of the Movies*. Garden City, N.Y.: Doubleday and Co., 1976.

A short introductory chapter very much to the point about making people laugh. Interesting sketches describing the work of the great Hollywood comedians from the Keystone Cops to Woody Allen.

Kelly, Elizabeth, *The Magic If: Stanislavski for Children*. Baltimore, Md.: National Educational Press, 1973.

Complete book of acting exercises based on the great Russian's theories. For children who want to really dig in. Starts from inner feelings, sensory work, playing actions clearly, creating characters, developing voice and body. Guide for teachers. Photos of two children doing many of the exercises.

McCaslin, Nellie, *Act Now! Plays and Ways to Make Them.* New York: S. G. Phillips, 1975.
Good suggestions on ways to get started making up your own plays. Ideas for theater games, dramatic situations, stories, puppets, dressing up, writing your own plays. Stimulating and easy to read. Glossary of new words.

Olfson, Lewy, *You Can Act!* New York: Sterling Publishing Co., 1971.
Good book for beginning actors. Many ideas for dramatic play, using body and voice, setting up scenes, and making up your own plays. Good notes for adults who might help you.

CREATIVE DRAMA FOR ADULT LEADERS

King, Nancy, *Giving Form to Feeling.* New York: Drama Book Specialists, 1975.
Personalized account of theory of using drama and movement with children. Great variety of specific exercises and activities using many points of departure.

McCaslin, Nellie, *Creative Dramatics in the Classroom.* 2nd ed. New York: David McKay Co., 1974.
Well-organized book for teacher beginning with drama. Sections on dramatic structure and building plays from stories. Good bibliography.

Spolin, Viola, *Improvisation for the Theatre.* Evanston, Ill.: Northwestern University Press, 1963.
Hundreds of theater games and discussion of principles behind game structure for improvisation work. Adaptable to many needs.

Ward, Winifred. *Playmaking with Children.* New York: Appleton Century, 1947.
Some useful pointers on using stories as the point of departure in creative drama work.

Way, Brian, *Development Through Drama.* New York: Humanities Press, 1973.
Excellent text for teachers and leaders who are inexperienced in drama; clear presentation of philosophy with many specific exercises.

COSTUMES

Jackson, Sheila, *Simple Stage Costumes and How to Make Them.* New York: Watson-Guptill Publications, 1968.

Survey of major historical periods in costume design, illustrated with photographs and drawings. Guide to pattern making for the more ambitious; good information on altering found pieces such as jackets and trousers.

Pointillart, Marie-Blanche, *Costumes from Crepe Paper.* New York: Sterling Publishing Company, 1974.

A full range of simple patterns for basic clothing shapes that can be adapted to many different specific costumes. Ideas could be executed in cloth for sturdier wear.

Purdy, Susan, *Costumes You Can Make.* New York: J. B. Lippincott, 1971.

Clearly illustrated instructions for elementary skills in cutting, sewing, gluing. Basic costume parts that can be fashioned to specific needs. Decorations and accessories. Simple and complicated versions.

Yerian, Cameron and Margaret, eds. *Make-up and Costumes.* Chicago: Children's Press, 1975.

Very simple suggestions for a huge variety of costumes and make-up designs. How to use available materials and clothing, adapt them to your needs, and unify the design. Deceptively simple, this book contains many sophisticated ideas.

SCENERY AND PRODUCTION

Cope, George, and Morrison, Phyllis, *The Further Adventures of Cardboard Carpentry.* Watertown, Mass.: Workshop for Learning Things, 1973.

Complete instructions for designing and constructing furniture, walls, "superstructures," stores, puppet stages, etc. from tri-wall corrugated cardboard.

Nelms, Henning, *Scene Design, A Guide to the Stage.* New York: Dover Publications, 1970.

For the more ambitious: detailed text and drawings relative to designing and constructing traditional scenery with flats and platforms as well as set-ups for working full round and three-quarters round.

Olfson, Lewy, *You Can Put On a Show*. New York: Sterling Publishing Co., 1975.

How to organize yourself and a group to handle the different tasks that go into putting on a performance for an audience. Describes the traditional way of dividing up the tasks in theater; different kinds of shows you could do; how to write your own.

Yerian, Cameron and Margaret, eds. *Stages, Scenery, and Props.* Chicago: Children's Press, 1975.

Excellent suggestions and instructions for making very simple, effective scenery and props. Pictures and descriptions of different playing areas you could use for your stage. Clearly illustrated throughout.

MUSIC

Faulhaber, Martha, and Underhill, Janet, *Music: Invent Your Own.* Chicago: Albert Whitman, 1974.

An excellent book for beginners; clearly and graphically explains fundamental elements of rhythm, timbre, melody, and dynamics; focuses on how to create your own music.

Hawkinson, John, and Faulhaber, Martha, *Rhythms, Music, and Instruments to Make*, Book II. Chicago: Albert Whitman, 1971.

Rhythms to walk and drum; instructions for making a variety of rhythm instruments, flutes, metallophones, xylophones, box harps, guitars, and violins.

Langstaff, Nancy and John, *Jim Along, Josie: A Collection of Folk Songs and Singing Games for Young Children*. New York: Harcourt Brace Jovanovich, 1970.

A good selection of traditional songs that could be used as written or altered to make new songs for *Silly Soup*. Notes on simple percussion accompaniment could be adapted for use with other songs as well.

Paynter, John, and Aston, Peter, *Sound and Silence: Classroom Projects in Creative Music*. London: Cambridge University Press, 1970.

An advanced book with ideas for using sound and music in many different ways. Sophisticated but filled with ideas that non-musicians can use.

C